FISHING'S GREATEST MISADVENTURES

Fishing's Greatest Misadventures

EDITED BY TYLER McMAHON & PAUL DIAMOND

Casagrande Press • San Diego, California

Published by Casagrande Press
San Diego, California

www.casagrandepress.com
casagrandepress@aol.com

Copy editing and book design: Steve Connell / Transgraphic Services
Cover design: www.liminalspaces.co.uk
Front cover illustration: Kevin Hand

Printed in Canada

    Library of Congress Cataloging-in-Publication Data

Fishing's greatest misadventures / edited by Tyler McMahon & Paul
    Diamond. —1st ed.
    p. cm.
    Includes bibliographical references.
    ISBN 978-0-9769516-4-3
    1. Fishing--Anecdotes. I. McMahon, Tyler, 1976- II. Diamond, Paul,
1970- III. Title.

SH441.F56 2008
799.1—dc22

                                2008033578

For Brother William Kendrick
and his fishing-obsessed sons:
Nathaniel, Ben, and Jonny

Table of Contents

NEAR-SHORE ODDITIES

A WORLD AWAY—EXOTIC FRUSTRATIONS

LAKE FISH: COMMUNIST COMPETITIONS, PRANKS, AND THE LAW

SPOOLED, SCARED, AND OUT OF LUCK

Introduction

TYLER McMAHON

I should probably make a confession: I'm not much of a fisherman. I wound up as editor of this anthology because the publisher liked my work on the book *Surfing's Greatest Misadventures*. My actual fishing experience is limited to two trips. Both took place in Montana, outside of Missoula. Both were made possible by my uncles, who live nearby.

Uncle Kevin, my mother's brother-in-law, took me on a summer hike in the Bitterroot Mountains with his friend, Forest. For several hours, we walked uphill along Chafin Creek. I wore inappropriate footwear and both my ankles were a blistered, bloody mess by the time we reached Tamarack Lake. I hadn't realized that Kevin and Forest both carried pack rods and spinning gear in their backpacks. As soon as they'd dropped their hooks into the water, the two of them reeled in one west-slope cutthroat trout after another. We piled the fish up along the bank. Even I could do it, once my turn came up.

Within minutes, we'd caught the limit. Kevin gutted a few fish with a pocket knife while Forest made a small fire. As if they were hotdogs, we roasted cutthroats on sticks over our makeshift fire, and ate them on the spot.

Years later, Uncle Tony, my mother's brother, took me on my second Montana fishing trip. He woke my cousin Chauncey and I up at 4 a.m. and loaded us into his car. We drove through the dark winter night toward Georgetown Lake, the headlights reflecting off fat flakes of snow, the wipers beating out a rhythm against the windshield. Tony passed around egg sandwiches and a thermos of strong coffee. With our heavy clothes and the car heater cranking like a furnace, Chauncey and I stayed drowsy despite the caffeine.

We parked on the shore of the frozen lake. Tony loaded us up with equipment—a manual auger, several buckets, three rods, two cases of beer—and led us out onto the ice. We made our holes, baited our hooks, sat on our buckets, and immediately started drinking.

In between beers and dirty jokes, we pulled in kokanee salmon and rainbow trout. Quite often, I'd have to walk away from the buckets and fumble through several layers of long-johns to drain a few cans of filtered beer out onto the ice. The snow muffled all the sounds and gave you the feeling that this vast wilderness was smaller than usual, flattened out and more intimate, like the lake and the mountains were all part of one big living room.

By noon, we had a bucket full of fish and another of empty beer cans. The snow finally stopped falling, and the sun broke through the clouds. We stumbled back to the car and scraped off the windows. At a restaurant nearby, Tony bought us all hamburgers, and bragged about the batch of smoked salmon he'd be starting on this evening.

In both cases, I have fonder memories of the trips themselves than the actual fishing. The blisters on my feet, the early morning beer buzz, and nature in all of its indifferent beauty were worth more than the size of the fish or the amount of the catch. I wouldn't trade either memory for any trophy trout or salmon dinner.

The stories in this book are remarkable not so much for the fish that were caught or the ones that got away, but for what these intrepid fishermen endured just for the privilege of casting their lines into known and unknown waters. In some ways, the privilege of what we endure is the truth that underlies fishing. We put ourselves at the mercy of nature, and await the unexpected with an open hand and a baited hook. This particular waiting separates fishermen from other people. While so many others anxiously plot, plan, scheme, and maneuver to get ahead or to get more by designing their futures, anglers wait silently by life's stream, preferring to reel in the actualities as they swim by.

What I learned from my two fishing trips and from my uncles is that there is no singular fishing experience. There are almost as many subsets of fishermen out there as there are kinds of fish. Sport fishing for marlin and noodling for cats are about as different as sunshine and snow. This book is unique in that it offers glimpses into many disparate points on the fishing spectrum. The narratives take us through a range of places and practices. The stories not only show the local color of the individual fishing cultures they reflect, but get at the fundamental commonalities which bind all of those angling subcultures together. Whether in Florida, China, France, Cuba, or Montana, fishing is always a matter of seeing nature not as something to be overcome but as something that can provide for us—whether our needs are food or recreation.

At its core, fishing is about our struggle to find something hidden, something deeper below the surface, something that doesn't always want to be found. As anglers, we come to the water like devotees to the temple; we come for fulfillment of hope and frustration. In these stories, the authors find themselves in the pursuit of fish. But in their pursuit of fish, the authors find themselves.

Noodling for Flatheads

BURKHARD BILGER

The great river was very dangerous [the Indians said]. There was a demon . . .
who would engulf any who approached in the abyss where he dwelt.
—Jacques Marquette (1673)

I have seen a Mississippi catfish that was more than six feet long and weighed
more than 250 pounds. And if Marquette's fish was the fellow to that one, he
had a fair right to think the river's roaring demon was come.
—Mark Twain, *Life on the Mississippi*

Growing up with Lee McFarlin, I never took him for someone with odd
and intimate dealings with fish. In our high school, in north-central
Oklahoma, Lee was one of those kids who sort of drifted from view: cutting classes and tooling around in his '62 Chevy Impala. When I looked
him up in my senior yearbook recently, he had a single picture to his
name—no sports, no clubs, no academic honors. Back then, the only
clue to his secret life was the faint tracery of scars along his forearms.

Late in the spring, when the rest of us were thinking about the prom,
Lee would head to the Cimmaron River. As soon as the chill comes off
the water, he knew, the catfish look for places to spawn. Hollow banks,
submerged timbers, the rested wrecks of teenage misadventure: anything calm and shadowy will do. Once the eggs are laid, the male chases
off the female with a snap of his jaws. Then for days he hovers over his
glutinous brood, waiting for the first fingerlings to emerge, pouncing on

any intruders.

That's when Lee would find him. Wading alongshore or diving to the lake bottom, Lee would reach into likely nooks and crevices, wiggling his fingers and waiting for a nip. When it came, he would hook his thumbs into the attacker's mouth or thrust his hand down its throat, then wait for the thrashing to stop. If he was lucky the thing on the end of his arm was a fish.

Now, your average catfish is an innocuous thing: farm fed, soberly whiskered, tender as an earlobe. But inflate that fish a hundredfold—like a flea seen through a microscope—and it becomes a true American monster. When it lunges from the river bottom, opening jaws the size of dinner plates, the suction may pull in almost anything: shrimp, fish, snake, or rat, baby duck or beaver. According to one old story, when pioneer mothers did their wash by a stream, they sometimes heard a splash and a muffled yelp: where a little boy had been playing, only a few bubbles were left.

It's been a long time since catfish were the stuff of children's nightmares—the troll under the bridge, the thing at the bottom of the well. But by all accounts they're only getting bigger. In the 1990s more than forty-five state records were set for catfish, including one for a 111-pound blue cat. People spear them with pitchforks or snag them with hooks spooled in by lawn-mower engines; some use boron rods with titanium guides, ultrasonic lures, or baits spiked with amino acids that seize control of a fish's brain. But a few, like Lee, still dispense with equipment altogether.

"I'll tell you what it feels like," Lee says. "You know little puppy dogs, when you shake the fire out of them when they're teething? That there's exactly how it feels." Catfish may not have fangs, but they do have maxillary teeth: thick rows of inward-curving barbs designed to let food in but not out. When clamped on your arm, catfish also have an unfortunate tendency to bear down and spin, like a sharpener on a pencil. "It ain't nothin' but sandpaper—real coarse sandpaper," one hand grabber in Arkansas told me. "But once that thing gets to flouncin', and that sandpaper gets to rubbin', it can peel your hide plumb off."

A second-generation hand grabber, or "noodler," Lee caught his first fish that way at the age of eight. Though the bite didn't break his skin, it infected him like a venom. He's married now, with two children and a plumbing business, but he still starts noodling when the wheat turns golden brown, switching to even bigger game at summer's end. His house, plain enough on the outside, is appointed in high atavistic style on the inside: heads looming from every wall, giant fish twisted in desperate poses, freezers full of strange meats. (Once, when a deer wandered through his sleepy neighborhood, Lee grabbed a hunting bow and chased it through his backyard.) Last spring, to make the place a bit more cozy, he brought home a baby bobcat.

Today, noodling with his family and me on a lake just west of our hometown, Lee needs less than five minutes to launch his boat, gun it across the lake, and leap into the water as we drift to a stop. A few seconds later he calls me over to a crumbling pier. "Sit here," he says with a weird grin, "I want you to feel something." I scoot onto the concrete, trying to look nonchalant. If Lee was enigmatic in high school, I was something worse: bookish, bilingual, taught to be terrified of the outdoors. ("The bones of drowned boys," my mother was fond of saying, "lie at the bottom of every farm pond.") While he was trapping muskrats and skinning wild pigs, I learned more about the American wilderness by reading James Fenimore Cooper in German.

Sitting on the pier now, I can feel reverberations of the old panic. Beneath me, all is quiet at first. But then, as Lee fumbles under the concrete with both hands, something begins to stir. Another dip of his thick shoulders, and the thing is fully awake, thrashing in the water six inches below me, thrumming the concrete with sharp cracks of its tail. We've found it—the troll under the bridge. All that's left is to reach down its throat.

The origins of noodling are difficult to imagine, much less prove. In North America archeologists have found fishhooks made of bone, weirs of wood and stone, and perforated shells for sinking nets. But noodling leaves no traces; it is as ephemeral as some of the boasts it inspires.

Native Americans, by all historical accounts, had a peculiar genius for killing fish. Hernando de Soto's men, trudging through swamps in search of El Dorado, saw lines of Indians splashing in pools, scaring up fish and whacking their heads "with blows of cudgels." Others men-

tioned Indians attracting fish with torches, lassoing them by the tail, harpooning them with lengths of cane, and drugging them with buckeye
and devil's shoestring. The most straightforward of all fishing methods,
however, was first described in 1775, by a trader historian named James
Adair:

> They pull off their red breeches, or their long slip of Stroud cloth,
> and wrapping it round their arm, so as to reach to the lower part
> of the palm of their right hand, they dive under the rock where the
> cat-fish like to shelter themselves from the scorching beams of the
> sun, and to watch for prey, as soon as those fierce aquatic animals
> see that tempting bait, they immediately seize it with the greatest
> violence, in order to swallow it. Then is the time for the diver to
> improve the favorable opportunity: he accordingly opens his hand,
> seizes the voracious fish by the tender parts, hath a sharp struggle
> with it against the crevices of the rock, and at last brings it safe
> ashore.

Most Indians, Adair goes on to say, "are in the watery element nearly
equal to amphibious animals." By contrast, the first Europeans to try
their hand at noodling must have been ungainly sights. Flailing out of
the water, gasping for air, they may have tried to do justice to the experience by rebaptizing it wherever they went. In Arkansas they called
it "hogging," in Mississippi "grabbling," and in Nebraska "stumping,"
though any given noodle might have two of three names for it. In Geor-
gia it became "cooning," in Kentucky "dogging," and in Texas and Oklahoma "noodling." "The way you get ahold of that fish," Lee explains, "it's
kind of like a wet noodle, squirming and squiggling."

As settlers drifted farther down the country's waterways, catfish stories sprang up with each new town and steamboat station. According
to one nineteenth-century report, catfish would congregate beneath a
dam on the Kansas River "like hogs in a hog lot," just waiting to be eaten.
Sometimes the same men who searched for drowning victims by the
dam would strap a gaff hook on one arm and dive for fish. At the turn
of the century a man named Jake Washington went down and came up
two or three days later—a drowning victim himself. "He hooked him a

giant fish and couldn't get loose," says Tom Burns, a self-proclaimed "old man of the river" in Lawrence, Kansas. "They found them side by side on a sandbar."

Since the great dam-building years in midcentury, American rivers have grown less hospitable to catfish. Brushy snags have been yanked clear, mucky bottoms dredged out, banks scraped clean, till the Missouri River, where some of the country's biggest blues once lurked, has become "a pretty swift ditch," in the words of one ichthyologist. If catfish have gotten bigger lately, it's partly owing to neglect: on the Mississippi Delta, where less than 20 percent of all streams could support fisheries in 1979, the Army Corps of Engineers has nodded off just long enough for some rivers to recover.

Like the black bears resettling once-ravaged parts of the Ozarks, noodlers may be an indicator species of sorts for healthy waterways. More often than not, though, modern noodlers are less throwbacks than thrill seekers, donning scuba gear, diving into reservoirs, and harvesting fish from made-to-order catfish boxes—a southern variation on lobster traps. (One noodling pond I visited in Arkansas had such clean, accessible catfish accommodations that it was called "hole-tel.") In Mississippi, once home to the scariest noodling waters in America, the sport's best spokesman in recent years has been Kristi Addis, Miss Teen USA 1987. One of her favorite pastimes, Addis told judges at the pageant, is grabbling for flatheads on the Yalobusha River. When pressed, she admitted that the mechanics of grabbling were "really hard to explain."

tick, tick, tick

I'm nostril-deep in murky water, sunk to the calves in gelatinous muck. Half an hour ago the troll got away, squirming through an escape hatch beneath the pier. A good omen? I'm not sure. Noodling, I know, is the fishing equivalent of a shot in the dark. For his master's thesis at Mississippi State University, a fisheries biologist named Jay Francis spent three years noodling two rivers. All told, he caught 35 fish in 1,362 tries: 1 fish for every 39 noodles. Still, it's too soon to take comfort in such statistics. From this vantage, Lee still seems dismayingly confident. Perched on the nose of his boat, surveying the shore, he looks like some raw country god, an embodiment of the lake: hair red as a clay embankment, bright puddles for eyes, patches of freckles like sandbars across broad, ruddy features. "Yessir," he shouts, "I guarantee you we're gonna find us some fish." On his best day, he adds, he caught thirty-five on this lake, all of them by hand.

tick, tick, tick

In the evening's honeyed light, the boulders and tumbled-down walls alongshore look ancient as Troy. "Used to be a gas station here," Lee says, wading toward a collapsed slab. "They love to hang out under this old sidewalk." Behind us, his kids have set sail from the boat in their water wings, like a small flotilla. "Daddy, can I ketch 'im, Daddy?" one of them squeals, bent on making me look bad. "You promised I could ketch one, Daddy." We shoo him away and take up positions around the rock, ready to reach in at Lee's signal.

tick, tick, tick

I've never been so aware of my fingers as I have been these past few days. I've found myself admiring them in pictures of myself, flexing them in the mirror, taking pleasure in their simple dexterity. Catfish, I've been told, share their love for calm, shady places with turtles, electric eels, and cottonmouth snakes. "In almost any small-town café, you can find some guy who says he knows a noodler who lost three fingers to an alligator snapping turtle," says Keith Sutton, a catfishing expert and the editor of *Arkansas Wildlife* magazine. His father-in-law, Hansel Hill, who has been noodling in rural Arkansas for forty years, had an uncle who once reached into a hole and found a "no-shoulders." The snake's bite left a permanent crook in his right forefinger. Some noodlers wear gloves, others probe holes with a piece of cane. ("If it feels rough at the end of that cane, it's a snake; if it feels like rock, it's a turtle," Hill says. "But that catfish is just as smooth and slick as can be.") Lee is a purist. Better to reach in with bare digits, he says, "so you know where you're at with that fish."

tick, tick, tick

"What the hell is that ticking sound?" Lee blurts, surging from the water for breath. "It sounds like a time bomb's about to go off down there." I glance blankly at him, still focused on my wiggling fingers. "That must be my fish locator!" some local yells from a nearby boat. He and his buddies have been floating alongside us for a while, hoping to get in a little rubbernecking before the sun sets.

"Well turn that damn thing off!"

Catfish have the sharpest hearing in the fish world: an air bladder tucked behind their heads serves as an eardrum, sending vibrations down an arch of tiny bones to the fish's inner ear. In Florida the Indians used to wear such bladders, dyed red, as earrings. I'm busy imagining this when I see something odd in Lee's face—a sudden tightening around the eyes. Then, just as quickly, his features relax. "You want to see him?" he says, jerking to one side involuntarily. I follow his gaze down. There, frowning beneath the water's surface, is an 8-pound flathead catfish, clearly disgruntled, gnawing futilely on Lee's thumbs. A homelier sight would be hard to imagine.

"Catfish are the redheaded stepchildren of America's rivers," Keith Sutton likes to say. "A lot of people think they're above catching them." My brother-in-law, George, who will fish for anything that swims, goes even further. Fish, he says, embody our social stereotypes. Haughty, neurotic, and beautiful, trout are natural aristocrats. Largemouth bass, omnipresent and resilient, are the river's working class. Catfish, in this view, are true bottom dwellers (though George says that gar, moon-eye, and paddlefish are even lower—piscine untouchables). It's an arbitrary ranking, based more on a fish's looks and personal habits than on its taste and fighting ability, but it can change the course of a river.

In the late 1980s the Army Corps of Engineers finally woke up to the untidy state of the Mississippi Delta. Twelve miles of the Yalobusha River, they announced, would be cleared, dredged, and snagged. "They said it would have no significant impact on the fish," Don Jackson remembers. "I guess they didn't think anybody would care enough to check." Jackson, then a newly appointed professor of fisheries and wildlife at Mississippi State University, decided to see for himself. Even the muddiest reaches on the Mississippi, he found, were alive with flatheads, channel cats, carp, and smallmouth buffalo. When he told this to some of his colleagues, however, they were less than impressed. That's just fine, they said, but what about the *real fish?*

Jackson and the Mississippi Wildlife Federation eventually forced the corps to scale back its plans. But most fishermen never bothered to get involved. It wasn't that they didn't care for catfish—even an ugly species can launch a thousand ships. According to the last national survey, nine million Americans catch catfish, more than fish for trout. "But the people running trotlines and hand grabbling are kind of backwoodsy," Jackson says. "They can lose things that are very important to them, and they still don't speak out." There is no environmental organization named Catfish Unlimited, no catfish-ecology chat group on the World Wide Web. Catch-and-release, an eco-religion of sorts among fly fishermen, is practiced by only one in fifty catfish fishermen.

To born-again fly fishermen—some of whom write laws for state fish and wildlife departments—noodlers rank even lower than paddlefish. Not only do noodlers kill their fish, they grab them at their most vulnerable moments, sometimes leaving thousands of eggs behind to be eaten by predators. The fact is, however, that noodling poses little threat to the environment. A single catfish can lay enough eggs to repopulate a stream reach. Besides, noodling is just too unpleasant to become very popular. "I can't tell you how tough it was," says Jay Francis, whose 1,300 noodles had less effect on catfish stocks than did the weather. "Some of those fish were just incredibly, incredibly vicious."

If noodling is legal in only seven states, the reason has less to do with environment than with ethics—and ethics of a perversely genteel sort. In the words of one ichthyologist in Missouri: "It's just not a sporting thing to do."

Stumbling across another muddy inlet, I have a hard time feeling sorry for the fish. In my right hand I'm holding a rope threaded through the gills of Lee's three catches, which swim along behind me like puppies on a leash. Blue cats have the worst bite, Lee says—"The difference between them and flatheads is like the difference between pit bulls and poodles"—but these flatheads look plenty tough to me.

A few feet from shore, the waves break across low, blue black humps, glistening beneath the water like a school of eerie, robotic fish. Two years ago Lee made these catfish dens out of sawed-up oil barrels. They were meant to be fully submerged, but the same drought that has been withering wheat crops in the Oklahoma panhandle keeps exposing these drums to the sun, forcing Lee to move them every few weeks. Wading

over to one, I see that Lee has his right leg inside it, struggling to pin
something against its inside wall.

"Owwwwwwww! That damn fish bit me!"

"Have you got him?"

"Not this one, that one! The one on your line!"

I glance down at my aquatic puppies. One of them has managed to
dodge through my legs, sneak up on Lee, and chomp on his big toe. A
bold feat, though hardly sporting.

"Hold on a second, just hold on."

By now Lee's eyes flash signals clearly as a lighthouse. He's found a
big one. In a beat I'm crouched next to him, arms tangled with his inside the den, hands splay-fingered to stop the fish's charge. Somewhere
in there, a fish is caroming off the sides of the barrel, ringing it like a
muffled gong. And I realize, with a shudder, that my fingers are waving
frantically, almost eager for a bite.

"He's on your side," Lee yells. "Can't you feel him?"

No, but how could I miss such a huge fish? A twitch of my right hand
solves the conundrum. I can't feel the fish, it seems, *because my arm is all
the way down its throat.* The fish and I realize this at about the same time,
like stooges backing into each other in a haunted house. The fish clamps
down, I try to yank free, and the rest is a wet blur of thrashing, screaming, and grasping for gills. At some point Lee threads a rope through its
mouth, and for just a second I get a good look at an enormous, prehistoric face. Then, with a jerk of its shoulders, it wrenches free, taking a few
last pieces of my thumbs with it.

Later, coasting toward our dock in the dying light, Lee guesses that
our catch weighs 25 pounds. Out of its element, though, it looks sadly
diminished: prostrate on deck, mouth working to get air, skin soft and
pale as dough. At first the kids scream when the boat hits a wave and
the fish slides toward them, mouth agape. Then the shock wears off and
their voices turn mocking, exaggerated. Finally one of them gives it a
kick: just another monster done in by daylight.

But not entirely. That night, when I come home from the lake, my
son comes padding down the hall to greet me. He's been hearing bed-
time stories about catfish all week—stories not so different, I'll admit,
from my mom's macabre tales. Now he looks up with anxious eyes as I

tell him about my day. And I feel a stab of recognition, watching his face contort with the effort of imagining. The troll, I think, has found a new haunt.

Amazon Sleigh Ride

KEITH "CATFISH" SUTTON

Despite its enormous size, the catfish cannot be seen in the coffee-colored waters of Brazil's Rio Negro. It is cruising the mid-depths of an 8-foot hole, swallowing every creature it can fit in its cavernous maw.

Minutes earlier, a 2-pound black piranha was its breakfast hors d'oeuvre. Now the fish waits, hoping to be served its main course.

When Bill Skinner casts a live piranha to the hole where the fish lays hidden, he immediately senses the invisible leviathan's presence. "My bait's going nuts," he says excitedly. "Something's down there."

The huge catfish sees the piranha and charges it like a killer whale going after a seal. The clicker on Skinner's reel screams when the monster takes the bait. Skinner engages the reel, pulls up slack and feels the 14/0 circle hook set firmly in the fish's jaw. Then all hell breaks loose.

Skinner's drag is set tight, and the fish uses his 130-pound braided line as a tow rope. We suddenly find ourselves on an "Amazon sleigh ride" as the gargantuan fish pulls our boat downstream. The whalers of old went on a Nantucket sleigh ride after harpooning a whale. We enjoy the Brazilian equivalent each time we set the hook in a big *piraíba*, a species many experts consider the toughest-fighting freshwater fish in the world.

Skinner looks at me and smiles. "*Grande!*" he shouts.

It is indeed a gigantic fish, and it fights gigantically. Skinner struggles to keep it away from the rocks. His rod bends so much I fear it will shatter. Skinner senses this, too, and loosens the drag. He soon regrets that mistake.

The *piraíba* surges away, peeling line from the reel at a sickening pace. In seconds, the spool shows through the few wraps of remaining line. Then I hear a sickening crack like the report of a small rifle. Two hundred yards of line are gone, trailing behind the one that got away.

As Skinner battled this monstrous fish, I couldn't help but wonder: how big is it? Unfortunately, I wouldn't learn the answer to that question. Although we hooked dozens of *piraíbas* during six days of fishing on the Rio Negro and its tributaries, we never landed one of the true giants. They straightened huge hooks, snapped heavy line like sewing thread and busted our rods. Some battles lasted more than an hour and a half, then suddenly the hook would come loose or some other mishap would befall us. Our hopes of landing a piraíba bigger than the current 256-pound rod-and-reel record went unfulfilled. The biggest we caught was a 100-pounder our Brazilian guides said was just a *filhote*—a fry, or baby fish.

The Tupi-Gurani Indians gave this giant catfish its common name, which means "mother of all fish." The appellation is appropriate, for the *piraíba* is one of the world's largest freshwater fish, with weights that can surpass 600 pounds, lengths approaching 12 feet, and a girth that can reach almost 5 feet. Its range includes large rivers in Argentina, Bolivia, Brazil, Colombia, Ecuador, French Guiana, Peru, Suriname, and Venezuela.

In his 1914 book *Through the Brazilian Wilderness*, former president Theodore Roosevelt was one of the first to describe the *piraíba* and discuss rumors that large specimens sometimes eat humans. "It is called *piraíba*—pronounced in four syllables," he wrote.

While stationed at the small city of Itacoatiara, on the Amazon, at the mouth of the Madeira, the doctor had seen one of these monsters which had been killed by the two men it had attacked. They were fishing in a canoe when it rose from the bottom . . . and raising itself half out of the water lunged over the edge of the canoe at them, with open mouth. They killed it with their *falcóns*, as machetes are called in Brazil. It was taken round the city in triumph in an ox-cart; the doctor saw it, and said it was 3 meters long. He said that swimmers feared it even more than the big cayman, because they could see the latter, whereas the former lay hid at the bottom of the water. Colonel Rondon said that in many villages where he had been on the lower Madeira the people had built stockaded enclosures in the water in which they bathed, not venturing to swim in the open water for fear of the *piraíba* . . .

Brazilians living along backcountry reaches of the Amazon still consider *piraíbas* a menace to unwary swimmers. "Perhaps they eat people; perhaps not," one native told me. "Are you brave enough to swim the river and find out?"

I was not.

Some baits used to catch *piraíbas* are as menacing as the giant catfish. Take dogfish, for example. The dogfish, or *traíra*, looks like a nuclear walleye. Dozens of nasty, needle-sharp teeth protrude helter-skelter from its massive maw. Its eyes glow like zombie orbs. The heads are chopped off and used as bait, and when I ran a 12/0 hook through the bottom lip of a half-pound severed head, it reacted in zombie-like fashion, chomping down on the hook—and nearly my fingers. A more wicked catfish bait never existed.

Unless, of course, that bait is a live piranha.

Piraíbas find live piranhas as succulent as filet mignon. Piranhas, however, have built-in razor blades for teeth. Hooking one properly behind the dorsal fin is like shaving with a shard of broken glass. You could lose a chunk of flesh in the process.

If you manage to bait your hook without mishap, you then must confront the dangers inherent in battling a heavyweight *piraíba*. The small boats used when fishing for them have no fighting chairs you can strap yourself in, and the possibility of being pulled overboard is real.

I have often tried to describe battling one of these giants in terms that lend a true understanding of their power. The best analogy I have found is this: Imagine standing beside an interstate highway and casting a hook that snags an 18-wheeler passing at 70 miles per hour. Now try to land that 18-wheeler. This is what it's like to hook a *piraíba*. I have landed 7-foot white sturgeons that rocketed from the water like Polaris missiles and 100-pound tuna that went on drag-screeching runs. Compared to *piraíbas*, they're sissies.

Some Brazilian fishermen have developed a novel method of catching *piraíbas*. A stout line is tied to the bow of a dugout canoe. The angler squats at the front of the dugout with baited line in hand, and when a fish strikes, he sets the hook and releases the line. If the fisherman is lucky, the *piraíba* will soon tire from pulling the boat, then the angler can paddle to the bank, secure his dugout to a tree and land the *piraíba* by pulling the line in hand over hand. If the fisherman is not so lucky, something extraordinary might happen, such as the incredible incident I witnessed one morning on the Rio Negro.

I was fishing with my friend Walter Delazari when I saw, about a half mile away, a dugout racing upstream. This was unusual, since the dugouts were rarely powered by outboards. I picked up my binoculars to get a better look and could see no motor. The only person in the boat—a small, older man—was crouched in the stern, his hands tightly gripping the gunwales.

"Walter, what kind of motor is on that boat?" I asked, handing him the binoculars and pointing toward the craft.

Walter looked. "No motoro," he replied. "Is *piraíba*."

"Quickly," I said. "Crank the motor and let's go. I want a photograph."

By the time Walter had the outboard started, the dugout was far upstream. We quickly closed the gap, but before we could get near enough to shoot a picture, the bow of the long, slender dugout was pulled under the water, the stern rose high into the air and the man was catapulted through the sky. The dugout then disappeared, swallowed by the great river.

The Brazilian had terror etched on his face as we pulled him into our boat. *"Grande piraíba! Grande! Grande!"* he shouted. Nothing we could do would calm him, especially since his dugout has not reappeared.

"Have you ever heard the story of Moby Dick?" I asked Walter as we motored away from the small village where we'd taken the old man.

"The story of Captain Ahab and the great white whale? This man we pulled from the water . . . do you think he is like Captain Ahab?"

"Actually he's much luckier than Captain Ahab," I said. "Moby Dick killed Ahab. That man is still alive and his Moby Dick is still out there somewhere towing his boat around."

Just then, a *boto*, one of Amazonia's freshwater dolphins, surfaced beside us and blew loudly. Walter and I were both startled.

"I know a place where we catch some leetle catfish," Walter said, smiling. "Today, I am not too happy trying to catch a big one."

I couldn't have agreed more.

Southern Hospitality

GENE CABOT

Like a lot of good old boys he'd been named after The General; everybody around Biloxi called him Rob-E-Lee for short. He lived across Back Bay by D'Iberville, and I'd see him around the Pass Christian Road launch ramp. From time to time we'd stop to talk fishing.

He was the only man I've ever known who chewed tobacco while smoking cigarettes. It was his belief that tobacco juice, if spit into either fresh or saltwater, would instantly make the fish stop biting. Based on this belief, he swallowed it.

"Why don't you just bring an empty beer can along to spit into?" I asked him one day.

"Shoot, if I see a beer can lying around on my boat, I'm liable to drink from it. This way, I cut out the middle man. Besides, it's only tobacco juice."

Since both of us had aluminum boats, our conversations frequently found their way back to metal boat maintenance. His boat was, to be polite, basic. About 18 feet long, dented and scratched, it had a lot of use behind it.

One day I noticed several silvery plates inside. Looking closer, I saw that they were aluminum patches, but the screws that held them were brass.

"These brass screws will corrode fast."

"You don't say? Have you got some of the compatible aluminum ones?" Rob-E-Lee asked.

"I think I have a few left."

"And you know how to do that sort of work?"

"Well, I suppose ..."

"Tell you what." Rob-E-Lee said, "If you provide the necessary tools and beverages, I'll hereby accept your invitation."

"What invitation?"

"To fix the damn patches in my boat. Isn't that what we're talking about here?"

Born in Chicago, I'd been moving around the States working on a series of air force bases. I liked Biloxi, especially for fishing. As the new guy in town, I figured I ought to consider this "invitation" a charming local custom, the southern equivalent of an Amish barn-raising.

A couple hours later, I sat inside Rob-E-Lee's boat in my driveway, removing patches. Under each of them was a smooth, round, dimpled hole about three-eighths of an inch in diameter. Rob-E-Lee wasn't tall, but his slender build and narrow face made him appear so. With such high cheekbones, I often wondered if he wasn't part Native American. He leaned on the gunnels and watched, one of my beers in hand.

"How did these holes get into the bottom?" I asked. "They looked like they were punched though from the inside."

Rob-E-Lee plugged in my extension cord and got himself a fresh beer. "They were indeed punched through from the inside. An old army buddy of mine, name of Billy Ray, came down from Laurel all excited about saltwater fishing. Seems he'd been reading quite a bit of them fishing magazines, and Southern hospitality dictated that I take him out, you know. But not wanting to wander out on the Gulf all day, I asked him how if he'd like to catch catfish, not bothering to explain the differences between fresh and saltwater cats.

"Turned out he liked catfish just fine. To impress him I offered a 6/0 outfit and took a level-wind for myself. I asked him if he could swim.

"He said, 'I used to paddle about a little but no, I'm not really able to get about in the water.'

"He'd grown quite a beer belly since the army days—I don't reckon he could see his belt-buckle whilst standing—so I figured he was buoyant enough. However, mindful that his heirs might make a fuss and tie me up in maritime litigation, I insisted he wear a life preserver as this here saltwater can get rough mighty quick.

"Billy Ray looked kind of puzzled, us only being out in the bay. But seeing I was serious and all, he finally put it on with a shrug. I had to point out to him that real tight strap between his legs was the belt, not a crotch strap.

"Well sir, we motored out toward Goat Island and I told him to put out that 50-pound navy anchor I'd snagged years ago. It is a bit big for this here boat, but the price was right. Billy Ray got it overboard with a few huffs. Damn near went over with it, sitting as he was with his feet in amongst the anchor line.

"I'd brought along some trout backs and told him to bury his hook well into one. His nose kind of wrinkled up, them backs being a couple days old, but he got it on. He looked around for something to wipe his hands on.

"'Just rinse them off in the water,' I told him.

"Billy Ray asked, 'Won't I risk getting them bitten off by sharks or barracuda?'

"I said, 'Well, yes sir, that is a distinct possibility. But your hands surely do stink, don't they?'

"He swished the tips of his fingers about, studying the water real close. I told him that it don't much matter looking, as you never see the fish that bites you anyway. He jerked his fingers up clean enough.

"I baited up with a small piece of trout, fished out two beers from the cooler and passed him a cold one. Leaning back on the motor I sipped mine and just relaxed, contemplating the wonders of nature.

"He kept cranking in that 6/0 to see if he still had any bait. I finally told him, 'Let it down, leave it down, put the click on and relax. But don't let go that 600-dollar outfit as there sure are some big fish hereabouts and if you lose it, you bought it.'

"Hold up," I interrupted Rob-E-Lee. "You valued that old 6/0 rig at 600 dollars?" I asked, knowing full well that lots better rod and 6/0 reels could be bought at the flea market for 100 dollars.

"Yes sir," Rob-E-Lee said with a straight face, "It has lots of sentimental value to me. Now, if you'll allow me to continue uninterrupted . . .

After four or five beers Billy Ray calmed down somewhat, but he kept asking me questions and making comments about all the exotic salt-water sea life hereabouts. Seems he'd subscribed to a bunch of those fishing magazines and memorized every damn story. That 6/0 clicked a bit, and I thought a crab might be making off with his trout back. I cautioned Billy Ray not to do anything, just let it go for awhile. Well sir, excited now, he gripped that rod with both hands and stared down into the water. Soon it was clicking pretty fast and I paid some attention. He just might have a fish on, for truth.

"'Okay,' I said, 'flip that lever, hold on tight and crank in. When you feel something, rear back and set the hook.'

"Well sir, he reeled in the slack and heaved so mightily that my stout pole doubled over. I'd have sworn he was snagged but the line paid out against the drag and cut through the water.

"'A shark! It's a shark! I knowed it!' he said. Give him credit; he cranked, bent, retrieved, and cranked some more. The sweat poured down his face and stung his eyes. I thought that old 80-pound test line would soon pop and he'd go overboard backwards. I was glad I'd made him wear that life preserver.

"Must've been cranking in and paying out line for more than half an hour when slowly up from the bottom comes this big stingray. I do believe that creature was 4 foot, wingtip to wingtip.

"He cried, 'I knew it! It's a devil fish! Help me get it into the boat.'

"'What for?' I asked, 'You want to get it mounted?'

"'No,' Billy Ray said. 'They're good eats. I read where you can skin those wings, rub them with cayenne pepper and garlic then cut off chunks to shish-ka-bob with onions and tomatoes.'

"Well now, I know they've been eaten and some folks say you can make a mighty good gumbo with them. But all the years I fished this bay I can't recall it being done around here.

"'It's too big,' I said, 'and that tail's got a real poison barb on it. Let's cut it loose.'

"'No!' he yelled. 'I want it! You gaff it for me.'

"'Not me,' I said. 'You want it, you gaff it.' I handed him that big old gaff I'd made from a rake handle.

"He passed me the rod and flailed away with the gaff. I thought he'd just pop the line and we'd be done with it. But, luck of the beginner, he snagged the gills of that there fish and heaved back hard. Big as a card table, that stingray slid up into the boat between us. Now I ain't never been jabbed with one of them barbs yet, and I didn't mean to get stuck then. I was quick up on the seat, watching him try to hold onto that gaff while that there stingray thrashed about with its tail. The ray wrenched the gaff out of Billy Ray's hands, and the handle swung around and hit me upside the head. I went down like a pole-axed bull.

"Billy Ray must've seen me falling down and then lying still in the bottom of the boat. I reckon he thought my life needed saving. Most of them good old boys carry protection, and it's often their first recourse in a crisis situation. He pulled out a snub-nose 38 and put all five rounds into that stingray laying there. That quieted it down but quick, and got my attention.

"Billy Ray asked, 'You alright?'

"'I'm not dead but I ain't fine by a damn sight.' I told him. 'Doing better than that fish of yours, anyway.'

"Above my ear, a big welt was already rising. I wanted to get ashore and away from Billy Ray and his stingray before anything else happened. I seen the bloody water rising in the boat, and hoisted that 50-pound anchor faster than ever before. At full throttle, I motored away from Goat Island while Billy Ray bailed water out. Thankfully, we made the launch ramp without sinking.

"Two of us dragged that bleeding stingray up the bank. Billy Ray dropped his tailgate and hoisted it in. Dirty and bloody, he pumped my hand like it was a well handle. He thanked me and said that he had to head back to Laurel directly, but he'd surely remember this day.

"As he drove off I stood beside my grounded, bullet-riddled boat and mumbled that I surely would remember it too. Look at me now: spending another weekend fixing this old boat, patching up these bullet holes that I didn't even make, for a fish I didn't eat, all so I could make an old buddy happy."

"It's a damn shame," I said. I wiped the sweat from my brow, then twisted hard on the last of the screws on the final patch.

"You're telling me," Rob-E-Lee said. He swallowed another mouthful of tobacco juice and fished a cigarette from his pocket. "When it comes to one's fishing gear and boats and the like, a man shouldn't be overly hospitable."

"Is that a fact?" I sat up in the boat and stretched my aching back muscles.

"It sure is." Rob-E-Lee breathed out a mouthful of smoke. "Say, you about done in there? That fridge of yours is nearly out of beer."

Letting Loose the Salmon

ANONYMOUS

The statute of limitations has not yet expired on my crime, so I can't mention the specifics of where I grew up and where these events took place. Suffice to say that my childhood home was on a bluff overlooking a beautiful harbor along the Pacific coast. Just after I'd started seventh grade, a powerful southerly storm roared through our area. During the gale a tugboat appeared in our harbor, pulling what looked like a big barge. I figured the tug was seeking temporary shelter from the storm before continuing on to a busy southern port.

A week later, the tugboat was gone but the barge was still in our harbor, secured by large buoys. I asked my father why a captain would leave a barge in the middle of the water. We took the binoculars out to our back deck to get a closer look.

"Those are fish nets," my dad said. "They're used to farm salmon."

He handed the binoculars to me. Through the lenses, I saw that the "barge" was in fact a series of ten above-water nets.

I'd spent my whole life on that harbor. My parents took me on long trips in our 30-foot sailboat. I had earned their trust enough to take our rubber dingy out and explore everything in range of the 2-gallon fuel tank. Nearly every weekend, my grandfather took me fishing for the different kinds of salmon that lived in the 48-degree water. Though I was only thirteen, I had years of fishing experience. I'd caught plenty of salmon on the hundred or more days of fishing I'd done with my grandfather. This harbor was my backyard, my playground. Seeing those metal cages out there was like finding billowing plumes of smog next to the soccer field or the sandbox.

After school one day, my best friend Habib and I went to get a closer look. We dragged the dingy from the high-tide wall in my backyard across several hundred feet of cobblestone rocks and into the water. Habib was thin and dark-skinned and had a huge, uncool Afro and a nose he had yet to grow into. He had recently broken his arm, and it was in a cast when he climbed into the dingy. Habib couldn't swim, and his mom had forbidden him, many times and in my presence, to get into boats with me. We motored across the water with smiles.

Up close, the pens were a series of aluminum posts that created a crisscross framework. Both the above-water and below-water nets were connected by lines to that aluminum frame. The nets rose above the surface and had net roofs to prevent eagles and seagulls from getting easy pickings. The air, normally sweet and salty smelling, was redolent of dead fish.

I counted ten pens. Each one was about 40 by 40 feet. Their perimeters were ringed by a grated metal platform attached to floating pontoons. We tied off to one of the pontoons. Habib stayed in the boat and kept a look-out for anyone coming, his arm-cast propped up awkwardly in front of his chest.

"I don't think we're supposed to be here," his voice came from the dingy.

"I've been coming here all my life," I said. "It's these pens that shouldn't be here."

I stepped onto the metal grating and looked into one of the pens and saw five, maybe ten fish floating belly-up upon the surface. The smell was horrific. Nothing about this felt right, fish being forced to live in cages. I looked closely into the water and saw thousands and thousands of fish, densely packed, teeming in a slow patchwork of moving spots.

I was silent as I looked around. A white plastic dock box sat nearby. I lifted the lid to discover, by smell and sight, that it was filled with rotting dead fish. Another white box contained pelletized feed. Next to that was a trash bucket, some Coke cans and candy wrappers lay inside. Ten-foot-long tubes filled with sand were scattered here and there—leftover weights of some kind. Habib was staring back at the shoreline a mile away, scanning the water for boats. We could see none in the twilight. On the deck, I found a rusted old gutting knife.

Habib was right. We weren't supposed be here, snooping around the fish pens. But without knowing anything about the science or economy behind it, I had an intuitive and undeniable sense that fish farming was wrong. For the first time in my life, I recognized that the adults—be they elected officials or captains of industry—didn't always know best. The world was not a black and white place, but rather a blurry landscape of overlapping gray areas. When I picked up the rusted knife and rubbed my thumb along the cutting edge, I was making my initial, clumsy stab at adulthood. My first and only criminal attempt to navigate the murky line between what was lawful and what was right.

I put a hand on a line attached to the aluminum frame and felt the tension.

"Dude, let's get out of here," called Habib from the dingy.

With the line in one hand and the rusted knife in the other, I sawed away. Habib turned back to the horizon looking for oncoming boats.

After a couple of minutes of sawing, the line popped apart. Oddly, the net below me didn't sag at all. I sat on the edge of the metal grating, put my foot on the net and pushed it down. A few fish escaped and I felt a rush. I cut three more lines, but the net still wasn't sagging. Finally, I realized that it had floats which kept it on the surface. It would take a long time to undo all the lines, then cut the floats off.

I had just started on the fourth line when I heard Habib yell, "Let's go!"

I turned and saw his arm extended towards a distant pier. A fast boat sped in our direction and honked its horn. I put the knife back where I found it and jumped off the dock into the dingy. We both got down low, so just our eyes were above the gunnels. The boat continued past us. We motored away in the opposite direction of my house, just in case we had been followed. We pulled the dingy up on the beach in the darkness.

Back in my kitchen, my parents asked what we'd been doing. I told them we went out to the pens and looked around. I didn't say anything about the rusty knife or undoing the net lines, much less about the boat that had come after us. My father told me that people in our community were upset about those pens and were fighting to get them out of our harbor. The biggest reason was that the effluent from all the fish smelled for miles, caused fish-killing algae blooms, and attracted hordes of barking, shitting seals. What's more, the fish were fed antibiotics, pharmaceuticals, and growth hormones which, along with the parasites and diseases that are particular to Atlantic salmon, would get into the local food chain.

That summer, after school had let out, my father and I took the sailboat to a far-off island. On the way we passed a large fish farm, about seventy-five pens. We motored close by and observed the massive production. Fish jumped everywhere in the pen before us, as a man in overalls and rubber boots threw pellets from his gloved hands. All those fish breaking the surface sounded like a waterfall. Seals were scattered here and there, some only a few feet from the nets, holding their bodies out of the water to get a good look inside. Sea gulls swarmed and screeched from above.

Summer ended and I started eighth grade. That fall another southerly came through. Before it had finished blowing, another tug showed up hauling fish pens—more than before and even closer to our house. The sight of them made me angry.

The weather cleared and Habib came over. It was a Saturday. His arm had healed. He didn't once mention the new pens in the harbor. For the rest of the afternoon, I did my best to distract myself. We played basketball in the driveway, then ping-pong in the garage. We used my parents' video camera to make a horror movie which ended with a shot of Habib's body and one of my mother's kitchen knives lying in the laundry-room sink, both covered in ketchup.

Once we'd exhausted all our standard pastimes, Habib innocently suggested that we take the dingy out to watch the sun set over the water. I agreed. While following Habib out the back door, I noticed the ketchup-stained knife in the sink. I stared at it for a half-second, then wrapped it in a rag and stuck it in the pocket of my jeans.

With the kitchen knife in my teeth, I stepped from the dingy to the floating dock, as my reluctant conspirator and less-reckless best friend said, "If we get caught, we are so screwed."

My heart pounded against my chest.

"Do you know what happens in juvenile detention places? You need to bribe your way out of your daily beating, and kids stab each other with sharpened toothbrushes."

I looked down at my feet through the grating. Underneath, thousands of Atlantic salmon writhed together in their confines. I took the first of the high-tension lines in my hand and sawed at it until it popped apart. I moved on to the next line.

"All you get to eat is oatmeal and fish sticks. And you go from the shrink to getting your ass kicked by the bigger kids. That's your day. Oatmeal. The shrink. And a black eye." As Habib sat in the dingy and catalogued life in juvenile detention as he imagined it, I hacked away until all the high-tension lines in the pen were severed. Still, the net around the sides had not sunk. I grabbed one of the sand-tubes, tied it to the top of the net and plunked it in the water. The net sank. Then I grabbed a handful of food pellets and threw it outside of the net. The salmon swarmed in an exodus that few anglers have seen. They leapt and jittered and fluttered into a new expanse. It sounded like the rushing of a class-four river.

I jumped up and down with a feeling of achievement that I had done something right and honorable.

To Habib's horror, I went from pen to pen repeating the process. In fifteen minutes, all the nets were sunk and the fish were free.

I jumped back in the dingy and took one last moment to look at and listen to the sound of the salmon slapping and flopping into the wild. The splashes sounded like "thanks" and "praise" as the pink sunset lent a color to my satisfaction.

Without lights, we motored in the opposite direction of my house. Once it was pitch black we headed home.

In the kitchen I boasted about our adventure to my parents. My mother's face took on a look of shock and fear. She yelled at me: "You have no idea what you've done," and "We can be sued!" and lots of other things. Over and over, she screamed that we could lose our house. Then she said she was taking us to the police station, that she had to turn us in.

None of these things had occurred to me. How was it possible that an act which caused such joy in my heart, which seemed so undeniably right, could upset my mother so much? The only thing I could do was assure her that nobody had seen us. Soon my father came home.

My dad called a lawyer friend, who gave him sage advice: "How do you know they released all the salmon? This community has been enraged by the fish pens for months. My firm is filling suit against the owners of the pens. Someone else may have been out there cutting those nets. I recommend that you not report this to the authorities. Your son could be held accountable for someone else's actions." With that, my father swore Habib and me to secrecy. Strangely, my dad seemed less angry than stunned. Now that I have a child, I understand that look of wonderment. It creeps onto my face when my child does something that is utterly beyond my imagination.

The next day, word spread of a fish-pen attack. It was on the evening news and on the front page of several newspapers the following day. One investigator suggested it was the work of a team of divers who planned the attack methodically and carried it out in the middle of the night. Another paper declared it an act of "Greenpeace-style" sabotage. Estimates of the value of fish lost were as high as $200,000. My mother clipped out all of the stories and hid them in her sock drawer, as if that might hide them from everyone in our community.

Secretly, the articles made me proud, even if my mother's anger and worry had eroded my sense of nobility. Now I was filled with the intoxicating pleasure of getting away with something that I wasn't supposed to do.

Throughout the month, local papers reported the ongoing investigation, the dire ecological possibilities of Atlantic salmon spawning in our area, and the new fishing opportunities. Cartoons ran on the editorial pages. One showed two fish in the water with a pellet floating on a hook. "What's that?" asked the Pacific salmon. The Atlantic salmon responded, "My food."

Reports claimed that fishing had never been better in our waters. People simply tossed in pellets and then scooped the fish up into their nets. The nearby river mouths and beaches teamed with anglers and "netters."

I walked to the river mouth near our house. From the bridge, I saw groups of people with nets simply grabbing 15-pounders from the water. The salmon were everywhere, and they had no idea how to act like real salmon.

It took a dozen years and several visits to campus libraries and the marine/fisheries department at my university before I realized the full consequences of my act. Setting the fish free had had an adverse impact on our local marine ecosystem.

Letting loose the salmon filled me with pride and shame in equal measure. The two emotions bleed together and feel indistinguishable to me—perhaps that's the consequence of conviction.

Chasing Trout

LAURAN DERIGNE

I finally met my Tarzan. While he didn't swing from branches, Garret could go days without a shower and he could spot ticks on me before they settled in. If I pointed to a tree, he told me what kind it was. And he could start a fire without using a bottle of lighter fluid. I couldn't wait for the years of adventure that lay ahead. Garret didn't have a single camping flaw. He proposed under the glare of his headlamp, one knee on an inflatable sleeping pad, and I said yes.

While some men stop doing dishes or the laundry once they're married, Garret stopped wooing me on camping trips. It started immediately after the wedding. Camping with my husband, it turns out, involves a lot of time chasing trout.

Don't get me wrong. We'd done some fishing in the years before we got married, and I enjoyed it. But I also relish the campgrounds nowhere near trout, where only blue gills dominate small creeks and trees are our sole entertainment—no 6 a.m. horn going off to signal the beginning of trout fishing, no chitchatting with fishermen wives in bathroom lines, and no fish guts strung along the hiking paths.

After we'd been back from our honeymoon for a while, I proposed a romantic camping trip—one where we could walk hand in hand along the river, have candlelit dinners at our picnic table, and watch the night sky for falling stars.

Garret stood in our dining room listening to me. He was still the dapper young guy I fell for five years earlier—his hair messy, not one strand of gray in it, and only the dimple on his chin, no wrinkles yet.

"I was thinking more of a fishing trip," he said. "Fish from dawn until dusk, come back to camp, grab a quick meal and hit the sack, sleep until early morning then do it all over again."

I didn't reply. My long frown and crossed arms said it all.

Finally, he sighed and said, "Sure, honey, whatever my wife wants."

The night before we were set to go, I found Garret in the basement with his tackle boxes. He wore his old Cardinals hat with the flies stuck to the bill. The Grateful Dead played from his worktable. He didn't notice me standing behind him with my arms crossed. I watched as he separated his dry flies, nymphs, and woolly boogers into separate compartments in his smallest fly case.

"What are you doing?" I asked.

"Just packing a couple things, in case you take an afternoon nap or something, and I have nothing to do."

"Right, good idea." I didn't hide my sarcasm. "We'd hate for you to be stuck outdoors with nothing to do."

As I walked upstairs, Garret bellowed, "Good night. I love you! Can't wait to pick wildflowers and sing songs around the campfire!"

I chose the primitive campground precisely because my guidebook specified that it was not frequented by RVs, barking dogs, loud car stereos, or rednecks slamming beers and igniting fireballs of lighter fluid.

It was quiet and beautiful. We hiked. We canoed through a lake where the fish were unworthy of being caught. We made a campfire, talked and drank beer. But the unspoken remained between us. His trout obsession hid below the tranquil surface of our camping trip.

On the third night of our campout, Garret flopped and flailed. He climbed out of the tent and opened the cooler. I listened to him drink a late-night beer, then heard the distinct rattle of fishing gear from the backseat.

The next morning I awoke to find him with the map out on the picnic table.

"Oh, boy. Here we go." I dragged my coffee-less body over to him and braced myself. The camping trip had ended, and the chase had be-gun.

Chasing trout required a change of campground. Trophy trout wa-ter is never close to the campgrounds I choose. Garret wanted to be so close he could see the fishes' every move from camp, so he could watch and say: "Did you see that one jump? They're going crazy out there. They must be hungry. Did you see that one? It was huge!"

We took down the tent, re-packed the car, and drove a couple hours to "probably the greatest stretch of trout fishing ever" and the camp-ground attached to it. The campground looked and smelled like the backyard of a fraternity house the morning after a keg party. Garret thought it looked just fine. I frowned and brooded over having to spend a night by a stinky bathroom that hadn't been serviced for months.

Trout campgrounds are notoriously crowded, messy and unkempt—men stay here. This one was no exception. The only available sites lacked shade trees. The fire pits were rimmed with melted plastics, rotten food, and fish heads. Squirrels grazed from the trashcans. I got out of the car and made a complete turn, looking for something pretty—a fern, deer, something . . . but I found nothing of beauty.

I frowned at Garret. The frown became a silent argument. We stood on opposite sides of an ashy fire pit staring at each other and volleying shoulder shrugs back and forth for 10 minutes. I intensified my frown so that it would embody all the disappointment of a failed first marital camping trip. Finally, my husband let out an exaggerated sigh, got back in the car, and slammed the door. I climbed in and stared out the win-dow. He tore past the campground's only tree, which happened to be dead.

We didn't speak for a while. At last, we crossed a bridge and saw a group of men fishing below. Garret turned to me and demanded, "Get the map out."

He stared at the map and chewed his lip for a good half hour, then resumed driving. We passed *Get 'er and Go*, a local convenience store, and stopped to ask about another campground in the area, pointing at the map in hand.

The attendant wore a T-shirt that read, *If I don't look drunk, get me another beer.* He explained, "Well, if you go up this hill to Highway K, turn right until you see County Road 365, turn by the yeller school bus parked in the field, follow that road for about 8 miles, and you'll get to Brown Bear Campground. It's a private campground; it'll cost you a pretty penny, but you're on good trout water."

An hour later, the map lay on my lap, folded into a square the size of a stamp—we were lost and out of our minds with frustration. I noticed a man laughing at us from his front porch as we drove by a dozen times in the hour. I made my husband stop the car so I could ask him what was so funny. He said that last week a loose bull rammed down the sign for country road 365 and now it rested in a ditch of tall grass.

Finally, we headed the right way. My blood pressure was dangerously high when we finally arrived at the Brown Bear Campground. An overly groomed man met us in the driveway and leaned into the window, inspecting the back seat, zeroing in on my husband's gallon jug of rum.

"Do you have any camping spots?" I asked, seeing nothing but one picnic table next to a bulldozer and a mound of dirt.

"Yep, we got one right there," he said, pointing to the same picnic table. "Or we got a spot there," he pointed to a fire pit next to the chained-up drooling Rottweiler by the side of his house. "But alcohol ain't allowed. Don't like to lose control of my campground. You'll have to leave that jug with me till you leave." He waited, eyeing the bottle of Captain Morgan's.

After a moment, he continued, "There's one more spot. You got to follow that mowed path through the field. It sits about 20 yards in. Skeeters can get bad there. You got some good bug spray?"

It neared two in the afternoon, and all we'd done was drive around all day. There was a nice cool breeze outside, but the passenger window didn't roll down. Stuck inside the stuffy car with the smell of wet socks coming from the back, I fell asleep, hoping to wake up back at the campground where our vacation started.

I opened my eyes and found us parked back at the filthy, smelly campground that we'd left hours ago.

At that point, my vacation was over. I grumbled, helped put the tent up, drank a rum and Coke by the fire, and stared up at the sky. I lay awake most of the night, listening to the squirrels scurry around our site, wondering if we were destined to be one of those couples that take separate vacations.

The next day I slept as long as I possibly could. Around 10 a.m. I unzipped, stepped out, and made a cup of coffee. Soon enough, I gathered the composure to head down to the river.

In spite of my intentions, I found myself smiling. The water was clear. The sun threw itself across the rippled current. Garret stood thigh deep in the water with his brown waders hugging his legs. I watched him whip the rod back and forth until the fly landed softly on the surface. It was a beautiful act to watch. He caught a trout, and it ran right and ran left, gave a good fight. Finally, he held it up and marveled, then turned to show me his catch. I gave him a thumbs up though I really didn't care. He looked as if he'd just won an Olympic gold. I watched for a while more, but decided not to linger. Over behind the bathrooms was a hiking trail that looked like it might lead somewhere deep into my thoughts about marriage.

As I started on the trail, I couldn't help but recognize that fishing is a lot like marriage. The perfect catch is often the one that gives you the best fight.

Death and Fishing

BILL HEAVEY

Did you ever have one of those days on the water when you happened to be in exactly the right place at exactly the right time and caught fish until you were sick of it? Me neither. I used to think I'd do pretty much anything to get a day like that. But when the chance came up this season, I passed it up. Twice, actually. Once was an act of simple economic self-preservation. The other, darker and more mysterious, involved death, a lawn mower, and the unspoken obligations a man takes on if he wants to look himself in the eye while shaving.

The first time, friends who are seriously dialed into the annual run of white perch up the Potomac invited me out. There are a couple of days a year when—tide, sun, wind, and thermometer aligning—the river may turn into a "silver tide," with schools of perch so thick that the water changes color.

"Tomorrow could be the day," Paula said. "Meet me and Gordon at the boathouse dock at 10 a.m." As a freelancer, I am absolute sovereign and master of my time. Until I am late filing a story, that is, at which point I turn into Chicken Little, sure that the evening sun will find me standing by the highway with the tools of my new profession: a squee-gee, a plastic cup, and a cardboard sign reading, *God Bless and Have a Nice Day*. Such being the case at that moment, I said I'd try to be down by 1 o'clock.

When I finally got there, I was told my friends had just left with a cooler full of fish. The tide was slackening, not a good sign for the perch fishing. But I was there, so I rented a boat, rowed into the current, and dropped anchor. I tied on a tandem rig of brown bucktail jigs with a 1-ounce weight, and something hit the moment the sinker touched bottom. Thirty seconds later, I had a jumbo flapping in the bottom of the boat. It was nearly a foot long, a meal in itself. I bumped its head on the gunnel and cast again. Ten minutes later, another. My hands were shaking. I couldn't believe this was happening. In an hour, six very big perch were splayed around my feet. It wasn't the silver tide, but it was the best perch fishing I'd ever had.

Then it stopped. I lost a few jigs in the rocks without even getting a bump and got back just in time to meet my daughter Emma as she stepped off the school bus. Filleted, lightly breaded, and fried, the perch made a splendid dinner.

It rained for two days straight thereafter, ruining the fishing and darkening my mood. Then word came that the mother of our next-door neighbor Dave had died suddenly. A routine checkup a month earlier had turned up a rare heart ailment. She passed away almost before she understood what was going on. After the funeral, Dave stayed on at her house for a few days to make some arrangements as her executor.

Meanwhile, the river had cleared, and it looked like I would get one last shot at the silver tide. Paula called. "Get your butt down here if you still want some perch. They won't be in for long." No longer on deadline, I headed for the car. Then I saw my neighbor's lawn, which had grown tall and lush almost overnight from the rain.

Like most people in the suburbs, Jane and I aren't really tight with our neighbors. We chat across the fence about our kids, but I don't think either family has had the other over for a meal in the ten years we've lived here. But I remember a day nearly eight years ago, returning home from the funeral for Lily, our daughter who died of SIDS one day shy of her fourth month. When we pulled into the driveway, Dave was there, his face wet and contorted in grief. He walked over and gave me a fierce, wordless hug. That had meant more to me than all the flowers and cards and casseroles we received in those awful days.

Now it was Dave's turn to absorb the hammer blow of sudden death.

And the first thing he would see when he pulled into his driveway to-morrow was an overgrown yard. I took my gear back inside, fired up the mower, and cut his lawn. It didn't take much time, just enough to miss out on the fishing. Dave had probably forgotten that long-ago moment, but it will stay with me forever. I was grateful to be able to repay the debt. As I finished, his wife, Beth, drove up with the kids. "You didn't have to do that, Bill," she scolded.

"Actually," I said, "I did."

Backcast

Excerpted from *Backcast: Fatherhood, Fly-fishing,
and a River Journey Through the Heart of Alaska*

LOU URENECK

Adam and I took our trip to Alaska the summer he graduated from high
school. I was forty-nine, and Adam was eighteen. I was deep into middle
age; he was on the verge of becoming a man. I had been divorced for
a year by then, though my former wife and I had been apart for three
years, in different cities separated by hundreds of miles. A chasm of
anger, disappointment, and sadness had opened between us. We communicated through lawyers. During most of that time, Adam and I had
lived together as father and son and sometimes as warring parties. I was
his custodial parent.

I had hoped that the trip to Alaska would settle some of the trouble
between Adam and me. It would be good, I thought, for us to go fishing
together one last time. In the woods and on the river, maybe we would
regain something of our old selves before he went off to college and on
to the rest of his life. Looking back, I have to admit the trip was a little
desperate. I had been willing to take the risk. My life was in a ditch; I was
broke from lawyers, therapists, and alimony payments, and fearful that
my son's anger was hardening into lifelong permanence. I wanted to pull
him back into my life. I feared losing him. Alaska was my answer. What

I had failed to appreciate, of course, was Adam's view of the expedition. For him, the trip meant spending ten days with his discredited father in a small raft and an even smaller tent. It was not where Adam had wanted to be, not now, not with me, and not in the rain. The trip would take us 110 miles of rugged Alaska, some of it dangerous and all of it, to us anyway, uncharted. I had no inkling of what lay ahead: fickle early-fall weather, the mystery of the river, and unseen obstacles that already were silently forming themselves in opposition to my plans.

As he was pulling out the last bag, Rick, our bush-pilot, stopped and pointed toward the head of the bay. I looked up. A young bear had come out off the puckerbrush and was ambling toward the lake and us. He seemed carefree and oblivious until the moment he caught our scent, or the scent of the mosquito repellent. He stopped short and peered toward us, snoot first, like a boy who had lost his glasses. He was about 5 feet tall, maybe 200 pounds. He wanted the fish in the lake, but we stood between him and the water. I couldn't tell if he could see us or just smell us, but our presence, however perceived, was causing him no small amount of distress. He turned in place and started toward us again. He closed the distance quickly on all fours, to about 200 feet. A bear can cover 200 feet in less than five or six seconds. Even a yearling bear can be dangerous, maybe especially dangerous. He's a kid with no judgment. I reached for my backpack and pulled out a can of bear spray. It was a pressurized solution of high-powered pepper juice that can shoot 30 feet and sometimes repel a curious bear. Of course, it can also make the bear madder than hell. I felt a little ridiculous holding the can in the air. It felt like a charge of oversize deodorant.

"Forget that stuff," Rick said. "I've got something serious for him."

He reached into the plane and pulled a leather holster from under the seat.

"Let's see if he gets any closer," Rick said.

For Rick, that many words in a row constituted an oration. The bear claimed a single step, and Rick slipped out a long-barreled handgun with a bore as big around as a butcher's fat finger. The bear stood high on two legs and looked fierce, stretching his neck upward, but he didn't advance, Rick raised the gun. I waited for a blast.

Damn, I thought. We are going to begin the trip with the killing of a bear.

It didn't seem like a good omen. Bears, owls, ravens, otters—killing some animals seemed like an invitation to disaster. Call it bad medicine. I had a friend, an archery hunter, who had shot a black bear with an arrow back in Maine. He told me how the bear, manlike, had gripped the arrow sticking from its chest and tried to pull it out. Crying and moaning, the bear went into a death scene worthy of opera. It lay down and clawed the ground and moaned. It rolled from side to side on its back and then staggered off into the woods. My friend gave up hunting bears. They were too high in the order of things. There was enough about this trip that was worrisome. I didn't want to add an insult to the spirits that hovered over the lake and river. Here was a dilemma: I didn't want to see the bear dead, but neither did I like the alternative of letting him get any closer. Bears killed people in Alaska. I had grown up on outdoor magazines with gruesome photographs of men mauled and eaten by bears. Rick held the gun steady. He clearly was a lot less troubled by the prospect of offending the spirits. One move forward and Rick was prepared to deliver the slug of the .357 Magnum cartridge somewhere to the left side of the bear's chest. We waited, and then the bear backed away on all fours. He took a broad arc around us and entered the lake 300 yards from the plane. Almost immediately, he hoisted a big sockeye against the gray sky.

"Well, Dad," Adam said to me. "Welcome to Alaska."

I took his words as a gesture of kindness.

I had coaxed Adam into this trip by telling him that Kanektok was probably the greatest fishing river on earth. I was sorry for my hyperbole. Since we had left Philadelphia, I knew that Adam had been searching for the flaw in my planning, and it was beginning to look to both of us like my screw-up was not forgetting the split shot, failing to pack an extra pocketknife, or leaving the instant coffee at home. I had achieved a first and, some might say, a pure impossibility: I had brought us to an Alaskan river where we would not be able to catch a fish. I kept my concern to myself. Had I staked this trip, and all that it meant, on the wrong river? Maybe I had. It was possible that we had arrived between pulses of the salmon runs and that the fishing had been phenomenal last week and would be phenomenal in another week or two, but that now it was nothing and we would endure ten fishless days. I had heard it from guides so many times before: "You should have been here last week."

I said to Adam, "The Middle River's what we want."

Maybe he would buy it. His face offered no clue.

For several hours, we floated and watched the landscape. We made cast after cast and got not a single strike to our flies. It was beginning to look for sure like one more thing that I had botched. After a long silent stretch, we switched places in the raft. Adam was sick of fishing—or rather, sick of casting. He took the oars, and I picked up a rod. I stripped line from the reel and let it lie on the floor of the raft as I worked the flex of the rod, back and forth. It was fun to be casting, even if I wasn't catching fish. I enjoyed the mechanics of the cast. The graphite spine of the rod was alive in my hands and responding to the way I worked it back and forth. It felt good, like standing in the batter's box and false-swinging a baseball bat. I took the rod through its familiar quarter arc, keeping my wrist stiff, and worked its resistance from my elbow and shoulder. I was in my sphere of pleasure, meditatively casting and not rushing the line in its journey through the air, when Adam spoke up.

"Dad," he said, "You're bringing the rod back too far on your back-cast."

I adjusted my backcast. It had been a little sloppy, for sure, and occasionally the line had caught the water behind me. I probably had played out more line than I could comfortably handle. I shortened the line by reeling some in, moved the rod through a tighter arc, and showed better control.

A little farther downstream Adam spoke again.

"Dad, you almost hit me with that fly."

I was fishing with a weighted fly, which tends to drop on the forward cast. It had zipped by our ears a couple of times. A weighted fly that smacks the ear or side of the head is painful and not uncommon when fishing in the wind, so I snipped it off and replaced it with an unweighted pattern. It didn't fish as well, but it was safer. I went back to casting. The fly swam just below the surface, above where the fish were likely to be in lie.

"You're not covering the water," Adam said.

I tried harder.

After a half mile more of river: "Dad, you're missing the best runs. You're wasting all the best water."

I could see that his criticism wasn't going to stop until I stopped fishing, and even then Adam would probably find a new failing of mine. He hadn't liked my rowing, either. It was too this or too that. I decided to overlook it: I was used to this by now. I knew it was my presence, and not my fishing, that was annoying him. Some of this has to be his age, I thought. At least I wanted some of it, a small piece of it, to be his age. Did it all have to be my fault? I knew that the parents of teenagers are pitiful and hopeless in the eyes of their children. I took some solace in the thought. In the last year, at various times, Adam had advised me that I had bad breath, thinning hair, body odor, a protruding gut, and that I slouched and made too much noise when I ate. Of the two parents, fathers are especially disgusting to children: They have patches of hair on their shoulders, and hair grows out of their ears and nose, they eat onions and sardines, and their toenails grow brown and cracked. One morning, I had made the mistake of coming out of the bathroom after a shower in my underwear.

"Dad, that's gross!"

Nothing was as vile to Adam as the sight of his father in his underwear. I had trained myself to chew slowly and quietly. I even swallowed with care. Adam had watched me across the kitchen table, listening.

"Nobody eats as loud as you do, Dad. I don't even know how you do it."

I kept a supply of breath mints. I sucked in my stomach around him. And I never, ever, went around in my underwear. As the parent of a teenager, I had learned to keep my capacity for being disgusting to a minimum. But there wasn't much I could do about my presence now. We were struck with each other in the raft.

"Dad, you're splashing the line on the water."

I took a deep breath. I figured it was time for us to take a break and have some hot tea on the shore. It was 7 p.m., so I might as well make dinner, too. The sun made a brief showing, and we beached the raft on a narrow gravel bar of white pea-sized stones that was sprouting willow bushes. I set up the stove and put some water to boil for hot tea and another pot for freeze-dried chili.

We were at a bend in the river that created a long, deep pool against a high bank opposite where we had beached the raft. The bank showed bands of colors, red and orange. It looked like some huge modernist painting, one horizontal bar of color blending into the next. Adam took his rod and started at the head of the pool, working it methodically downstream as if it were a Cartesian plane. This was the way he had been taught by the French-speaking guide I had hired when we fished the Margaree River in Canada four years ago. We had made that trip at the end of the summer before Adam had entered high school. It was our last trip before I separated from my wife. As I watched him working the pool, I recalled how the guide, Robert Chaisson, had stood with Adam in the river, shoulder to shoulder, and showed him the importance of covering all the water. The fish could be lying anywhere, and the beat we had been fishing was too valuable to ignore any piece of it. Adam began with short downstream casts and lengthening them in increments, a yard at a time, sending the curve of the line in sweeps over every bit of water as it slid by in a flat plane from the head to the tail of the pool. There was not a piece of river bottom to which he didn't expose the trailing fly, a No. 2 Black Leech. He had not forgotten the lesson that Robert had taught him on the Margaree. That had been a good trip. Life then had been simpler for Adam and me.

As I pulled the box of tea bags from one of the packs, Adam, who had worked his way down to the pool's exit riffle, let out a shout.

"*Dad!*"

He had a fish on. The rod bent almost to the point of snapping. The fish appeared hooked well, and Adam was trying to turn its head and move it out of the fast part of the current. Adam knew how to fight and land a fish, and he was playing this one with skill, though it still had the better of him. It rushed out into the heavier current and stripped line off the reel. The key to playing a big fish is to tire it so it can be beached or netted without breaking the line, which tapers to an almost-invisible hundredth of an inch, light enough to fool it into striking in the first place. Fishermen use the rod's bounce and the reel's two-way spool, which lets line out as well as takes it in, to absorb the fish's struggle and prevent the line from snapping. The more it struggles, the more it fatigues, and the force applied through the rod and spool is never more than the tensile strength of the line. Eventually, the fish lacks the strength to continue the fight, and it can be brought to hand or shore. Playing a fish is a form of jujitsu. It is a contest that rests on a single cruel irony. One of the combatants has knowledge that the other lacks: the futility of struggle. An old, smart fish understands the game. It changes the rules and even the game. It will not fight back. It holds in the current, confounds the fisherman and stalemates the battle.

For the skilled fly fisherman, the art of fighting fish is this: to balance the loss of the fish from a broken line against the death of the fish from exhaustion. A fighting fish expends enormous amounts of energy and oxygen as it strains against the resistance of the line, rod, and reel, taking it to the edge of death and sometimes over the edge so that it floats lifeless to the boots of the fisherman. Its fate is in the hands of the man holding the rod. I had taught Adam that it was better to lose a fish than to kill it.

Adam had taken naturally to the lesson. I had been bringing him along fishing with me since he was five or six. If he wasn't searching for frogs, he would sit patiently on a rock, Gandhi-style on his heels, holding a landing net and waiting for me to hook a fish. When I brought one to my waders, he would splash over to me in his sneakers and shorts and slip the net under the defeated fish. He always insisted on its release, alive and unharmed.

"Let it go! Let it go!"

From the beginning, when I first put a rod in his hands, at age seven in a brook near our home in Maine, he had fished with intensity but without aggression. It was a rare combination in a good fisherman. I had known lots of good fishermen. Many felt the need to land and kill every fish they hooked, and some weren't happy until they took every fish out of a stream. It was their aggression that gave them focus. They were fish killers. Adam's focus came from another place. I don't know that I had ever seen him happier than the day, when he was about six years old. That he discovered a nest of baby mice in the barn. He called me out to see them, full of wonder at their hairless pink bodies, each small enough to curl up on a penny. He watched them for an hour before I insisted that we cover them back up with duff for their mother. He had that same look each time he caught a fish.

Another day, he ran into the house as I was reading the newspaper, eager to show me what he had caught in the clover in the front yard. He thrust out his hand. I looked closely over my newspaper. Pinched between his thumb and middle finger was a fat bumblebee, furiously pumping and straining its stringer.

"Adam," I had said slowly, "don't let it go. Let's walk to the door. Just hold it carefully. When I tell you to, and not a second before, throw it out as hard and fast as you can. Then stand back because I'm going to slam the door."

It was easy to turn him into a fisherman. I just put him near water.

Adam had been what parents call an easy child. He had not fussed much as a baby, and as he grew up, his early easiness developed into a gentle nature. He took the world as it came to him, and he sought ways to accommodate himself to it without antagonism or conflict. Even now, a lot of what he was angry about, I guessed, was the fact that I had made life difficult for him by causing him to be angry. He was angry at me for putting him in the position of having to be angry. He saw me as the cause of his distress, and of course he was right. He had loved living his life inside our family. When he was small, he made gingerbread houses with his mother at Christmas and he liked to set the table at Thanksgiving. Each setting had a paper turkey or Pilgrim with a name on it: Mom, Dad, Elizabeth, Yia Yia, Uncle Paul. In the sixth grade and eager to please his older sister, Adam had let her relieve her boredom one night by dyeing his hair green in the bathroom sink.

Of course, he also had a maddening side: He was constitutionally incapable of hanging up his clothes or putting anything away or taking a shower that lasted less than forty-five minutes and required no fewer than three large bath towels, and he had a stubborn streak. His stubbornness was now fixed on me as the person who had torn apart our family.

I watched him fight the fish. He was knee-deep in the river and his line was tearing across the pool. He was tall, loose in his long limbs, and muscled in his arms and shoulders. He had his mother's high cheekbones and light complexion. He held the rod saber high as I had shown him when we had fished in Maine. It gave him leverage over the fish in the strong current. Yes, watching him, I had to acknowledge the extent to which I had come to value my life through my children. They were good kids, Adam and his older sister, Elizabeth, and they gave me—or I selfishly took from them—a handhold on a better sense of myself.

As he waded deeper into the river, I saw in my son a person who would go farther and be more than his father. I didn't want him to have my life: There had been too much hurt in the beginning of mine. Things had gone wrong. I wanted something better for him, and I wanted to break the curse that I felt had been set down on me. Yet I had put all of this at risk. In the last few years, I had met many men who no longer had any contact with their children because of a divorce. These men didn't see their children at holidays and missed their graduations. They seemed bereft as they told of learning secondhand about their children's careers and weddings. I couldn't bear the thought of losing my son. I wouldn't let it happen, even if it meant taking the risk of a self-guided and under-financed trip to Alaska.

After a prolonged battle with the fish, too long really, Adam brought its heavy flattish body to the beach; it was a sockeye salmon. It had a big green head, fierce hooked jaw, and blood-red body. It looked like a demon cut from the top of an Indian totem pole. It was downright scary lying there on the beach, gasping for air and pumping its tail. The fish hadn't sought the fly; it simply had been snagged as the fly passed over it. The odd hookup accounted for the long fight. It was a wonder that he had landed the fish at all. It hadn't been caught in the right way, for sure, but still it was a fish. And not just any fish, it was an Alaskan salmon, an honest-to-goodness Alaskan salmon, and it was our first fish of the trip.

Hallelujah!

For a few minutes, we were on top of the world. I took a picture of Adam: my son and his fish in Alaska. He knelt with the fish and held it forward with both hands toward the lens of the camera to make it appear even bigger. He was smiling. I was smiling. This was what I had been hoping for: a father-and-son moment. Maybe this trip was going to work out after all. We were back in the old groove, celebrating over a big fish. For a moment, our troubles fell away. I snapped several more pictures, and then Adam cradled the fish in the water until it swam out of his hands and disappeared in the deep channel. We drank our tea sitting on the edge of the raft and ate our chili, satisfied that with our fishing prowess and overall excellence as men of the wilderness, and then we set back onto the river.

On the second day, as Adam and I came swirling around a bend we encountered a sow brown bear standing knee-deep in the river. She was with her cub. This is the most dangerous way to meet a bear. A startled she-bear with a cub is a guaranteed exception to the rule that bears tend to leave you alone if you leave them alone.

She was fishing, looking down into the water and swatting salmon out of the current. Her pig-sized cub was on the bank, watching her. For the cub, it was both lunch and a life lesson in salmon fishing. For Adam and me, it was a serious no-shit situation, very possibly deadly for us or the bear, and even as we realized it, the current was bringing us nearer to her. She was unaware of our silent approach on the surface of the water. The river was moving swiftly, with a slim channel down its center. The edges of the river, right and left, were shallow and rocky, so if we held our course, we would be forced to pass within feet, within claw-reaching distance, of the big female. There was no way to run the raft past her. She would surely attack. At a minimum, the slash of her claws would deflate the raft, turning it into a waterlogged rubber pancake. We would be splashing in the water with a thousand-pound bear as our gear floated downriver.

I decided quickly to beach the raft and pulled hard on the oars to reach the meager shoreline. Adam reeled in his fly and stowed his rod at the bottom of the raft. I tried to row the raft upstream even as I headed to the nearer edge of the stream. I feared that an attempt at landing on the opposite shore, away from the bear, would carry us farther downstream and a few lethal yards closer to her. The raft scraped onto the sand and rocks, only about 40 yards upstream from where she stood. In bear terms, this is absurdly deep in the danger zone. A brown bear can cover the distance in three seconds or less. In spite of their size, bears are fast, quicker even than Olympic sprinters. So there were, in clear view, not much more than one hundred paces downstream, and on the same side of the river as the big sow. I heard my heart pounding in my ears.

I hoped that once we beached the raft she would spot us, see that we were not a threat, and amble off into the bush. Already, though, I was pulling the shotgun from the lashings on the stern. I took two lead slugs from my pants pocket and dropped them into the gun's two chambers. I closed the gun. It clicked. The bear looked up but not toward us. She didn't seem to know where the sound had come from. Then Adam stepped from the raft. At the crunching sound of his foot pressing down on the gravel, she looked toward us. My heart rose in my chest. I held my breath. Up until we beached the raft, Adam and I had been exchanging a string of variously low and modulated "holy shits," with him encouraging me to get the damned raft to shore as fast as possible. But we had gone silent on the shoreline. I didn't know whether our voices would warn her off or startle her into attack. The sound of the boot on the gravel fixed our position for her.

She put her porcine eyes on us. The air congealed. She lumbered from the water but maintained eye contact. She was enormous, probably 9 feet tall, and her Paleolithic architecture showed through her heavy coat. When she walked, the giant triangular plates that were her ursine scapula shifted under the carpet of her pelt. She was long through the body and neck, with a massive head and prominent snout. It was a head big enough to fill a basement freezer. She stood up straight, pointed her nostrils into the air, and grunted. It was the amplified sound of a heavy chest of drawers being pushed across a wood floor. *Rrrruuuggg. Rrrruuuggg.* This I guessed is what a wild boar sounded like rooting for food. She rocked from side to side. She had seen us, and now she was trying to get a better sense of us through her most acute sense, smell. I hoped we didn't smell like fish or whatever the pheromone was that communicated fear. I could hear her breathing, a kind of windy whale sound travelling through long church-organ pipes. The sight of us obviously was a taunt to her, a challenge. Would she rush us? Would she attack? The instinctual belts and pulleys of her big simple brain apparently were at work, calculating distance, smell, shape, and movement. She was making up her mind.

I joined Adam by stepping out of the raft, ever so gently. All of my motion was away from her. I was careful not to make a move that was toward her or that appeared fast or aggressive. I gripped the shotgun in my left hand. I reached back into the raft and pulled out one of the long cans of aerosol bear repellent. I pushed the gun's safety into the firing position.

"Hey, bear." I spoke quietly at first. Then more loudly, affirming my identity as a human. "Hey, bear. Everything's okay, bear. No problem, bear. Just a couple of fishermen, bear." It was the voice I would have used had a mugger stuck a gun in my ribs back in Philadelphia: "No problem, man, take what you want. Here's my wallet. Just don't kill me or my son."

Ashore, Adam started to walk upstream on the thin strand of beach, away from her, and she got back down in the water to watch him. She was fixed on him, not on me. Was that because he was in plainer view? I wasn't sure what our next move should be. Now it was my parental mind that was making its own set of calculations.

My brain plotted the position of the bear, the cub, me next to the raft, and Adam behind me and walking upstream. It was a rectangle that could have easily fitted within the bounds of a tennis court. I felt myself move upward into a state of hyperalertness. Suddenly I was aware of everything around me, and all my senses sharpened. I could taste the metallic saliva in my mouth. I felt the size and shape of my tongue. I felt the wind on my face. It was moving from the bear to us. It lifted the tiny heart-shaped leaves of the alders and showed their lighter undersides. A small black bird, catapulted from upstream, shot between the bear and me and disappeared into the thicket, I heard the river gurgling, the wind moving through the bushes, and her breathing and grunting. Once before I had felt this level of superawareness: My car had been rear-ended by a tractor-trailer on the Maine Turnpike in a snowstorm. In the three or four seconds that it took for the car to flip over and land on its roof on the embankment, my mind filmed the scene in all its detail: two oncoming cars, the snow in the funnel of headlights, the *whoosh* of the truck's brakes from behind. And then a blast of its horn, the guardrails, the car turning over in the air, the deafening boom as the car came down on its roof, and the subdued crunch of the windshield.

The bear was rocking and grunting, and I noticed that the fur low on her body was darker, where it was wet. Her forearms seemed short for her long body, and twice she came down onto them but pushed herself back up into her erect and towering posture. We were without a place to retreat. The upstream beach narrowed and then disappeared, where the alders met the river. Adam walked away faster from the raft and then broke into a slow jog. The bear came down on all fours and moved toward him. She stopped and then moved again, a bit faster, splashing in the water.

"Adam," I shouted. "Stop."

My voice didn't turn her eyes from Adam. She seemed locked on him the way a missile locks on a plane. It was clear that the bear was reacting to his retreat. He just wanted to keep moving away from her, and I felt the same almost irresistible urge to run, but it was moving away that was bringing her on.

"Adam, stop," I shouted again.

The opportunity to shoot before she went into a full gallop was disappearing. She was only 25 yards from me now, and I could smell her. It was the smell of a Labrador retriever that had been rolling in dead fish. Adam was still moving. If the bear were to reach him and attack, I knew that he knew to put himself into a ball and lie still on the ground. The victim of a bear attack could sometimes survive by playing dead and allowing the bear to bat him around. There would be flesh wounds, maybe worse, but death might be averted if the bear felt that its prey was no longer a threat. Adam knew this, too, but he also knew enough not to run away from a bear. He knew that running triggered a predatory response. Knowing and doing in these situations were two different things.

There was no question I would fire those slugs into the bear's chest if I had to, and it was looking as if I would have to. I was reluctant to shoot only because I was afraid that I wouldn't kill her. I certainly didn't need a wounded bear on my hands. What the hell would I do then, fall on her with my Swiss Army knife? Yet she was closing in, and I could fire a shot in the air to try to frighten her off, but if that failed I would be left with a single cartridge.

The shotgun was loaded with magnum-sized slugs. Packed with a heavy load of powder, the slug, a full ounce of lead about as big around as a spool of thread, would exit the muzzle with hundreds of foot-pounds of force. If it struck the bear, it would tear a big hole, break bones, and sever arteries. But that might not be enough to ensure her death. I was unsure that I could deliver a killing shot, even at this close range. A shotgun lacks the spiral scores, or "riflings," in the barrel that make a rifle's bullet accurate over distances. Shotguns have smooth bores, and they are made for firing loads of shot—multiple pellets—that cover a big circle. They are meant for shooting small flying things, like ducks. Slugs fired from a shotgun are powerful, enough to push an engine block, but wildly inaccurate.

I could fire at this bear and the slug might strike her chest, or it might miss by a foot or two, hitting her gut or paw or nothing at all. A shotgun is a point-blank weapon. If I wanted to be sure of placing a killing shot to her chest, I would have to wait until she was almost on me or passing me as she went for Adam. At a distance of 5 or 10 yards, I could fire directly at her and hope that the lead slug would break through the cage of her heavy ribs and explode her heart. It would be like firing into the grille of an oncoming car. The engine might go dead, but the car would still be moving. I would have to stay cool and place a second shot before she landed on top of me, dead.

I prepared to shoot. I had no other choice. I would fire the right barrel first, then the left.

I shouted one more time.

"Stop!"

This time, Adam brought himself under control. He came to a halt. The bear stopped, too. She stood and watched us both, bringing me into the line of her vision by moving her head rather than shifting her eyes. She grunted, rocked some more, and then looked back toward her cub. The action was now stopped, but the scene might not be over. What would she do? I looked down the line of the barrels. The bead was on her chest. She was grunting but not moving. She looked downstream. Her cub had disappeared into the willows on the left bank. Mother bear looked back to Adam, then back for her missing cub. The big simple brain was making a new calculation.

I held off on firing. I waited for her decision. One step in our direction and I would gently press the trigger. My decision was made. I waited. She was angry, damned angry, and clearly she had intended to attack. Yet another impulse was tugging at her. It was her maternity. Her cub was nowhere in sight. She turned, splashed her way back to the fishing pool, and climbed the bank. Adam sprinted back to the raft, and we hopped in and pushed off. Adam took the oars and rowed ferociously downstream, hugging and brushing the opposite bank. We passed the place where she had been fishing with no sight of her in the brush. I was still in a state of high alert. I drank in the sight of each leaf along the stream, the sparkle of the sun on the river's ripples, the clouds scudding overhead. I felt exhilarated, delivered, and sick in my stomach. My skin was tingling.

"Damn," Adam said, shaking his head and leaning back as he pulled hard on the oars. "That was close."

"Too damned close," I said. "Let's get the hell out of here."

The river maintained its narrow course. It seemed to have gotten narrower, and it was continuing to make blind left and right turns. There was a chance we would face a repeat of the situation we had just left behind, maybe with the same bear.

We went several hundred yards before either of us spoke again.

"We need to be extra-careful through here," Adam said.

"I'm thinking the same thing," I said.

"Do you have something, a pot or pan or something, I can bang as a warning?"

I dug into the cooler and took out a saucepan and a big spoon. I clapped them together as we floated along.

"Hey, bear," Adam sang out. "Coming through, bear."

I was feeling a little giddy.

"Do you realize how goddamn close that was?" I laughed.

I thought of the bear joke my brother had sent me as an e-mail when I was planning the trip. I told it to Adam.

"It seems that the Alaska Department of Fish and Wildlife was working up a new warning to fishermen in bear country. It still told them to wear bells to avoid startling a bear and to carry pepper spray in the event of contact. But the new warning also said that fishermen should know the difference between the paw prints and scat of black bears and grizzlies. A grizzly's paws are larger, and its claws are longer. Black bear scat contains berries and rabbit fur. Grizzly scat has little bells and smells like pepper."

"Very funny, Dad. Ha-ha." He drew out each of the last two syllables. "Ha-ha."

Aussie Sleigh Ride

DAVID FINKELSTEIN

South Australia boasts a disproportionate number of fanatical shark fishermen. That's understandable, perhaps, because one of the best places to catch a big great white like the star of *Jaws* is at Dangerous Reef, an aptly named rocky outcrop just a few miles off the country's south coast, close to Adelaide and Spencer Gulf.

While most anglers in the area stick to tamer pursuits—fishing for drummer, whiting, tuna and such—some are driven by an almost obsessive desire to boat the most vicious and feared of sharks: the white pointer, as it's known down under. One of the most persistent of these sharkaholics is Rolf Czabayski, a retired electrical contractor who immigrated to Australia from the former East Germany. Rolf is a cheerful and good-natured man, built like a bulldog, with an oval faced, blue eyes, and an ever present smile. In four years of trying he had hooked into four monstrous whites and lost them all. It was the last of the four that the 64-year-old remembered most clearly. A slight glitch in the usual procedure almost finished him.

It was a fine (Australian) summer day in January when Rolf, accompanied by his faithful deckhand, left the marina at Port Lincoln, motored out to Dangerous Reef in his 35-foot launch, and began laying down a chum slick—a practice called "burleying" in local parlance. Soon a giant white pointer followed the slick to its source. As often happens with this fishing method, the monstrous shark swam up to the boat, stuck its head out of the water (well above transom height) and opened its gaping, tooth-filled jaws to be hand-fed, seemingly as docile as a pet dog. The white pointer devoured each huge hunk of seal instantly as it was plopped into its open maw—at the time, the International Game Fish Association had yet to ban the use of seal (or other mammal) flesh as bait—and greedily returned for one helping after another.

Standard operating procedure requires that after stimulating the shark's virtually insatiable appetite, the angler then places a baited hook in its big mouth, and Rolf did just that. The great white had been sufficiently humored; now the moment of truth had come.

Rolf scrambled into the fighting chair, which was mounted on top of the engine hatch in the cockpit. He locked up the reel, and leaned back in the chair in anticipation, his outstretched legs braced hard against the footrest. Now prepared to do battle, he signaled his deckhand to hit the throttle. The boat roared forward, so as to make doubly certain that the shark would be well and truly hooked.

The only problem was that the engine hatch on Rolf's boat was hinged at the stern end and opened from the front; and, more to the point, it had been inadvertently left unlatched. Apparently, after checking the oil at dockside, Rolf's deckhand had neglected to put the securing bolt back in. So when the boat steamed off in one direction and the great white shark headed off in the other, the engine box sprang open, and the astonished angler suddenly found himself catapulted rocket-like high over the transom of his boat. Still firmly harnessed to his heavy bent-butt rod and Penn International 130 reel, he sailed through the air for a few fateful seconds, then crashed into the water and disappeared.

Rolf plummeted headlong into the sea, smack into the middle of his erstwhile chum slick. An involuntary submariner weighed down by his equipment, he found himself slicing through the water, pulled by a great white that was busy trying to shake the hook from its mouth. Rolf did not meet it face to face, which surely would have put a quick (but gory) end to the angler's career. Instead, the powerful fish swam steadily ahead, towing its tormentor along in its wake.

Blinded by the sting of salt in his eyes and choking on the torrent of water that flooded up his nose and into his mouth, Rolf was unable to breathe and had to act quickly to save his life. He struggled to find the drag lever of the Penn. When he released the reel into free-spool mode, he slowed his forward motion, but he began to sink rapidly under the weight of all his gear. Miraculously, he managed to release the buckles on his kidney harness. As he kicked frantically through the rays of light toward the surface, he took one last look at his rod and reel descending to the bottom. Now all he had to worry about was the angry and enormous shark in the vicinity.

The deckhand, seeing Rolf disappear into the distance and then sink suddenly out of sight, threw the engine into reverse and hit the throttle hard.

With the surface in sight, Rolf kicked and pulled with arm strokes, fighting to get there before unconsciousness or the shark got him. He broke the surface, took a breath, then heard the whirling props of his boat bearing down on him. Suddenly, he wished his harness had taken another second to unbuckle. The propellers cut into his flesh and inflicted injuries so grievous they would have made the white shark proud.

Though he had no way of knowing it at the time, his exploits would later gain fame down under as the Australian version of the New England "Nantucket sleigh ride" of yesteryear (in which a dory full of New Bedford whalers was towed at great speed and in considerable peril behind a harpooned whale). The Czabayski version differed in two major respects: he had left his dory behind, and the leviathan towing him was not a whale but a very angry great white shark.

When I spoke with Rolf in Adelaide several months after the incident, he was still recuperating from his wounds. His right arm was badly scarred from the severe lacerations inflicted by his prop.

I asked him how his recovery was going, but the fearless shark fisherman only wanted to discuss his next trip to Dangerous Reef. He invited me along.

Despite the accident, Rolf surprisingly had not fired his deckhand. He seemed to have forgiven the deckie both his initial screw-up and his panicked reaction in backing the boat right down on top of him, thus adding injury to insult. I thought about asking Rolf if on his next trip out it would be the deckie's turn to fish, with Rolf attending to the engine bolt, but I decided not to, which left a brief moment of silence in our conversation.

"Hey," Rolf said, filling the pause, "I'm looking for a volunteer to dive Dangerous Reef and retrieve my rod and reel." He explained that the exact whereabouts of the rod and reel were of course unknown, but it was likely the shark in question would have stayed around Dangerous Reef for a good long time. The shark would have swum along the bottom, through rocks, snapping the line, and the hook would quickly have become dislodged, or been rotted away by acids in the fish's mouth.

I politely begged off, saying I wouldn't be voluntering because my ears were bothering me at the time.

Though he never found his lost rod, Czabayski's persistence did pay off. Several years later, he hooked and boated a 1,102-pound great white on 50-pound tackle. By so doing, he joined the ranks of the IGFA's prestigious Thousand-Pound Club, and its even more exclusive Twenty-to-One Club. He now captains the *Calypso*, a charter boat that takes tourists and scientists out to view and study the behavior of white sharks.

Fit to be Tied

BOB T. EPSTEIN

In 1993, Captain Scott Stanczyk of Islamorada, Florida, took his charter boat, *Catch 22*, to Isla Mujeres off the coast of Cancún for the tremendous sailfish and white marlin fishery in the spring and early summer. Scott and his brother Richard invited me, as they had several times in the past, to fly down for a week and take some action billfish and dolphin photography. Normally, I flew round-trip on Mexicana Airlines, where the passengers clap upon landing. This time, instead of returning to Florida by air, I would be riding back on the 48-foot *Catch 22*. Sometime before we passed Cuba, I would have to take my turn at navigating (which I wasn't looking forward to that much, as my skills in that area are limited).

I showed up for the grand finale of an epic fishing trip. In its two-and-a-half month stay in Isla Mujeres, the boat already racked up an amazing 500-plus hookups on fly and spin gear. To add to the excitement, the senior mate—we'll call him "Mike"—had recently learned that his wife was cheating on him. The day before my arrival Mike got properly drunk and met an attractive local gal. He proceeded to wine, dine, and bed the lass. In the morning, Mike awoke from a drunken stupor to discover that his date was more than he'd bargained for, and a lot more than he'd noticed last night. She was a he.

Mike rushed from the room, got sick to his stomach, and then told our captain about it. Being only human, the captain radioed home to discreetly tell a close friend, but he made the mistake of speaking over an open frequency. The entire fishing community of the Florida Keys went on a laughing binge at Mike's expense.

Mike's strategy for dealing with this embarrassment was the same one he'd used in handling his marital issues: to get deeply and irredeemably drunk. He was still on his round-the-clock bender when I arrived with my camera, anticipating a fun fishing trip up the Caribbean.

The day I arrived, the crew suffered another setback when Richard Stanczyk fell and seriously injured his back, landing spine-first on the edge of the salon step. After a few days in bed, Richard stoically resumed fishing, though he still appeared to be in terrible pain. Despite the drama and the injuries, the fishing was to die for.

On our departure day from Isla Mujeres, a catatonically drunk Mike made the slurred announcement that he would jump overboard and end his life in the blue water off Cuba. He could not face the shame of everyone back home, nor did he want to continue with his life. None of us could contemplate the idea of sailing him toward suicide, and we couldn't trust him to take a plane home in his current state. So we found a solution. Following our captain's lead, we wrestled Mike to the ground and bound his hands and feet with rope. Deprived of the ability to bring liquid to his mouth, he'd have to sober up a little, we thought.

And so, as our drunken buddy screamed and begged to be untied, we left in late afternoon on a glassy ocean. The smooth and beautiful swell was punctuated every so often by a myriad of flying fish, frightened by our steady advancing bow. We even got a shot at a 90-pound white marlin along the way, but we missed the hookup.

Night fell over the smooth, eerily green water and a canopy of stars appeared above us. I settled in for some sleep before my late watch at the wheel and was gently rocked into a dream of catching the biggest fish ever on a fly rod.

At 2 a.m. I was woken by the captain ordering everyone to the cockpit. We were being boarded by the Coast Guard, who were checking for drugs, contraband, or smuggled Mexicans. A group of helmeted young Coast Guardsmen looked us over and unscrewed some overhead ceiling panels.

One of the officers went over to Mike, who was tied up in the corner of the salon. He stood over him and said, "Sir, are these men holding you against your will?"

"That's right," Mike slurred. "I want to jump overboard, but these bastards won't let me."

The guardsman looked back at me, "What's with him?"

"He's recently divorced," I said.

"Why is he tied up?"

"He got it on with a she-male by accident in Mexico, and now he wants to kill himself." I said. "I'm surprised you guys didn't hear about it over the radio."

The guardsman looked at Mike and asked, "Is this true?"

"He spoke the truth."

"This is a damn mountain of paperwork right here," he said. "Do me a favor. Don't untie this guy until you get to dry land."

Satisfied that we were not smugglers, they replaced the screws and reboarded their brightly lit cruiser. Their boat shone like a faceted gem in a calm phosphorescent sea as it motored away.

As were off once again Mike quipped, "Ha, they couldn't even find my vodka stash!" I tightened his ropes, and we were on our way towards the Cuba passage and eventually to Key West. As my watch began, the breeze had already turned to a freshet. The seas were up. The men went down to take their turns sleeping in the berths. I was captain for the middle of the night shift.

The weather turned bad, and fast. Rain blew like nails at the boat. I stood at the helm while these nails hit my face at 45 miles per hour. There was so much water on my seat that I couldn't stay on it. 25-foot seas lifted and dropped the boat, making it damn hard to stand and hold the wheel. The water on my cheeks felt intermittently cold and warm. I saw my life flash before me. I cried for my mother, my wife, and my kids. As a sailor and navigator, I was the least experienced of everyone aboard. But I was not about to go below, crying in fear to ask someone else to take my place. I did stomp on the fly bridge deck to summon someone up to help me steer; nobody answered my call.

The waves continued to grow. They were reaching 30 feet—out of my league. I felt as though I were trying to drive the boat the wrong way around a cutting saw blade. If we didn't hit a rocky island or another boat, I feared that I might take a direct hit from an oncoming wave and possibly fracture the hull. Each time the boat fell down a passing swell, I thought I heard the sound of cracking fiberglass. We couldn't take many more hours of this punishment. And I couldn't navigate this boat in the storm.

Then I heard a sound from the stairs on the fly bridge, a thud that was somewhere between a step and a stumble, and a voice said, "I can handle this, Epstein."

It was Mike. He had managed to untie himself, and while his blood-alcohol level likely remained high, there was an intensity in his eyes that told me he was genuine. This was a man who had decided upon death, looked it straight in the eye for the past couple of days. He had nothing left to fear.

Suddenly, I had my own catch 22 aboard the *Catch 22*. I stared hard into his intense eyes, "How can I trust that you aren't going to take us all down with you?"

"I'm going to get us out of this jam!" he screamed into the stinging rain.

I was so grateful that I hugged him, but he pushed me away. "None of that shit. Get downstairs, Epstein! I'll take it from here," he shouted.

I looked back at him in one last attempt to gauge his sincerity.

"Go on. I can jump overboard later. If I'm going to die, I sure don't want to see you assholes in the afterlife."

Soaked through and bone tired, I fell in a heap on the floor of the salon and slept without dreaming. I was eventually kicked awake and offered the helm once again, this time in much calmer seas. The storm had passed, and we were some 13 miles off the western tip of Cuba. Mike had taken us safely through the storm. Nobody made a big deal about it, but I knew damn well our lives had been in peril. It's just the way of seasoned boatmen not to talk about mortal possibilities (though the captain later told me privately that he too had worried we might not make it through that night).

After my second shift, I was asked to keep a sharp eye out for a blue marlin that Richard Stanczyk was hoping to hook for a record on the fly rod. Seems that every year, in about the same area off of Cuba, Captain Scott noted that a blue marlin of extraordinary size would show itself on the teasers. His brother Richard had waited the entire trip for this moment. I took the helm while the others were in the salon having a snack.

A large fish showed up behind the teasers. I couldn't make it out in the brilliant gold early morning light that rippled off the waves. It looked like a big old dolphin so I called it a dolphin.

"Are you sure it's not a marlin?" asked Richard Stanczyk.

"Yeah!" I said.

So Captain Scott turned to the second mate and yelled, "Toss a ballyhoo at it, we can use some fresh fish fillets."

The second mate did so and promptly hooked up a perfect blue marlin—his first.

The fish wasn't the big one, but it definitely could have been a world record on the fly rod. Richard was livid with anger and disgusted with me. When he saw the marlin launch in fighting leap, he wanted me overboard. He'd lost his one and only shot at a blue that he might have captured, measured, and photographed for the record books, then released. The rest of the trip home Richard just kept muttering, "that dumb Epstein."

Finally Key West hove to, and what a great sight that bit of land was to me and all aboard. When I saw the outline of the island, I imagined what it must have felt like to see that land for Haitian refugees, or the passengers of old sailing hulks that depended on wind power alone.

We tied up at Key West Marina and didn't wait for the customs check-in. We were too hungry. We went for a hamburger and our first fresh-brewed coffee since leaving Mexico.

When we returned to the boat, a customs officer was waiting, ready to fine us. I think the officer briefly mistook us for Cuban asylum-seekers when we stumbled over toward him. Our hair was caked together, our skin covered in thick layers of salt, and—to his alarm—we all reeked of diesel fuel. A 55-gallon barrel of fuel had opened on us during the rough part of our passage. Initially, the odor on our skin had made us sick, but we'd gotten used to it.

After looking us over and checking out the boat, he felt sorry enough for us to settle on a warning. We headed to Islamorada and home.

After two hot showers and two eight-hour shifts in a solid bed, I was startled awake by a call from Richard.

"Bob," he said, "Would you believe that your dumb call on that blue marlin probably saved my life? When I had that fall in Mexico, turns out I broke the third transverse vertebra in my spine. The pain I had was the broken edge knifing at the nerves of my spinal column. The doctor says that had I fought a blue marlin on the fly rod, I probably would've driven the sharp-edged vertebra shard through the nerves and into my spine. Which would have paralyzed me, at least, and very probably killed me right there out on the ocean. So I'm calling to thank you and your dumb-ass move for saving my life."

In the months that followed, Richard made a full recovery from his injury. Mike saw through his divorce and eventually entered rehab for his drinking. He's now happily remarried and a fishing guide in his own right—a darn good one, as I'm told.

As for me, next time I plan on flying back to Florida, and clapping along with the rest of the passengers as we land.

Out of the Blue

BY IAN CARD (WITH COLIN KEARNS)

When chasing marlin in the Atlantic, you could wait all year for conditions like the ones we had—calm seas, clear skies, and wind at 5 to 10 knots. As my father motored the 40-foot *Challenger* through glassy water, I looked at the fading silhouette of Bermuda 10 miles in the distance.

Four of us were on the boat: Alan, my father and the captain; Leslie, the angler; Dennis, a friend of mine along for the ride; and me, the balding, bearded, thick-framed mate. This was the morning of the Sea Horse Anglers Club Billfish Tournament with a $78,000-first-place prize. At about 8:30 a.m. we dropped six lines in the water and trolled at 8 knots.

The bite started steady and stayed that way. We hooked a white marlin and pulled it off. We missed another white, then hooked and lost a fish that fought like a small blue. It was almost 11 a.m. when the big blue crashed the spread.

As soon as Leslie set the hook, the reel started screaming. Nobody had to say it, but everyone aboard knew that we were onto a trophy, a fish that could take first place. My father stood in control at the helm. Leslie worked it from the fighting chair. We were into our rhythm, and things were looking good. The marlin, and the contest, were ours to lose.

Just ten minutes into the fight, Leslie's line went from screeching to slack, and he couldn't reel it back fast enough to find tension. The fish had changed direction and was charging the boat. It's exactly the way that seasoned, cunning marlins tend to get loose of the hook. My father pushed forward on the engines to put some distance back between us and the marlin. But it kept coming, chasing us down, faster than we were moving. Then the water buckled and broke and the 14-foot fish leapt over the transom in a great arc.

I was standing in the cockpit. I remember seeing the fish in the air, just for a moment, flying over the right corner of the stern, sunlight reflecting off its slick body. I remember trying to side step out of the way. And then the world went black.

The fish had speared me at the apex of its leap and then carried me 15 feet in the air, before drilling me headfirst into the water with all 800 pounds of itself driving me under. Either the initial impact of the bill, or impact of hitting the water knocked me momentarily unconscious. I'm not a small guy; I've got wide shoulders, a thick chest, and a low center of gravity. I'm not used to being thrown overboard or tossed about like a rag doll by a fish or a human, which says something about the power of that marlin.

The crew lost sight of me as soon as I went in. They say my arms were wrapped around the fish, as we crashed into the water. Then it thrashed its tail and carried me deeper, out of sight. Somebody wisely cut the fishing line.

At some point soon thereafter the fish shook me free of its bill, and that's when I woke up underwater. All around me the sea was blood-red. I panicked and furiously swam the 6 or 7 feet to the surface. The boat was 50 feet off and backing up toward me. I took my first few desperate gasps of air. I made the choice to look at the boat approaching me instead of all of my blood spreading out around me. Once the boat was close enough, my father and Dennis each grabbed an arm and lifted me in.

Blood was pumping out of my back as Dennis lay me down on the deck. I'd been stabbed just above the collarbone with enough force that the bill exited my back just below the shoulder blade, my spinal cord spared by an inch. Dennis took one look at the exit wound and quickly stuffed a towel into it. Then he applied pressure to my shoulder wound. He did all of this in silence, while Dad raced the *Challenger* toward shore.

It wasn't pain that I felt. More like as a strange pressure with the odd sensation of a foreign object having been in a familiar place. The exit wound was as big around as a fist, a tunnel carved straight through my shoulder by the 3-foot bill. Blood drained through the towel onto the deck.

No one said a word to me during the ride. But Dennis's tortured face hovering above mine spoke volumes. It was impossible to say how much blood I'd lost. I knew from the silence that the trip back to dry land was a race for my life.

Though I felt no pain, only a dull sensation in my right shoulder and arm, I wondered if I would survive. Ten miles never seemed so far. I was scared and shocked. How could my life come down to something like this? Standing in the wrong place at the wrong time, when a big fish happened to jump. Shouldn't there be some greater design or meaning behind my death? A good cause, a courageous risk with some profound last words, perhaps?

After a forty-minute ride, we were met by an ambulance at a service station. At the hospital, they performed some X-rays to check for bone damage, and I underwent extensive surgery to clean and stitch up the wounds. I was able to go home a week later, with nine stitches in my chest and five in my back.

Take your index finger and draw a line straight down from your right eye to just above your collarbone. That's where the marlin's bill entered. Now, put your finger in the middle of your shoulder blades and move it just to the right of your spine. That's where the bill exited. I have a 3.5-inch scar in my shoulder and a 1.5-inch scar in my back. If the fish had hit me one centimeter to the left, the bill would have severed an artery. A half-centimeter to the right and I would have lost feeling in my right arm.

In the days and weeks that followed, I received calls, letters, and e-mails from all kinds of people, from close friends and family to customers who chartered trips with my father and me years ago. Other than some numbness and discomfort in my right arm, I've had an almost full recovery.

These days, I don't think about the accident too much. I don't play it over in my head or have nightmares about it. It hasn't turned me off marlin fishing. If anything, I now appreciate a perfect catch even more, considering all that could go wrong. Every single day out on the water, each time I set the hook or pull the leader on one of those powerful fish, it all feels like another blessing in a life that was given back to me when that big blue shook me free of his bill.

Marlin Catches Man

MARY L. PEACHIN

Alaskans Paul and Donna Claus went honeymooning in Tahiti, but soon grew restless. Sipping cocktails in unbearable heat wasn't their idea of the perfect vacation. A few days along, as they sat side by side on deck chairs, looking into each other's blue eyes, Paul said, "Let's get out of here. Let's go fishing in Hawaii." They called their buddy Glen Van Valin in Kona and made fateful plans to spend the rest of their trip as a three-some, fishing for big marlin.

Glen kept his 26-foot Wellcraft, *Karma*, docked at the Kona marina. Eager to see his newlywed friends, he offered to take them on a multi-day fishing trip. He picked them up at the airport that evening, and a glorious sunrise welcomed them the next morning as they set out into the Pacific.

Just as they cast out the lines, before lowering a teaser or snapping into the outriggers, a huge marlin struck. Paul scrambled into the fighting chair and set the hook. It was just past 6:30 in the morning.

The fish broke the surface in tail dances, thrashes, high leaps, and other attempts to spit the hook. Veteran anglers, Paul and Glen estimated the fish weighed between 800 and 1,000 pounds. Then the marlin made a run for it, peeling line off the reel so quickly that it smoked. Glen put the boat in reverse, and still the fish stripped the line to the backing, quitting its run just shy of the end of the line.

This was no ordinary hook-up. This marlin was not just huge, it was also pissed off. Paul managed to bring it to the boat four times in two hours, but the marlin wasn't ready, and Glen wasn't about to consider gaffing a thrashing, 1,000-pound fish that still had plenty of fight left in it.

The *Karma* had a slightly unorthodox setup for its fighting chair. For better fish scanning, Glen had fastened the chair on top of the engine cover. Glen's ever-cautious, hazard-evaluating brother-in-law had helped him strengthen and enforce the attachment chair by adding eight steel bolts from the chair into the engine cover. They attached a car seat-belt for stability.

When the marlin struck, Paul got in the chair and put the seatbelt on, but didn't have time to get properly situated in his harness. He managed to get into it and secure his rod to it, but he never tightened the straps.

After another hour of back-wrenching reeling, Paul hauled the monster to within leader-length of the boat for the fifth time. As the fish came near, Glen grabbed the flying gaff and yelled, "Donna, hold the wheel of the boat in an arc!"

Glen leaned over and took a closer look at the fish, trying to gauge if it was green or ready for the gaff. Paul had been fighting for over four hours. He held fast to the rod in case the fish made any unexpected moves.

"Get ready. I'm gaffing this fish," said Glen.

Paul unbuckled the seat belt that held him snug in the chair, as Glen swung the flying gaff toward the water. A flying gaff is a pole with a detachable hook at the end. That hook is typically secured to the boat with nylon line. Once the hook is set in the gill, the fish is tied to the boat on a virtually unbreakable line and can be more easily hauled aboard. The nylon line in this case was tied to Paul's chair.

Donna came out of the cockpit to watch Glen set the gaff. As Glen touched the marlin's gill with the business end of the gaff, the fish exploded in a blur of thrashing fins and flying water. Then it ran, and as it did a loud crack rang out, and Paul and the fighting chair were launched into the air. The bolts that held the chair to the engine cover glimmered with reflections of the morning sun. They were still attached to the chair as it cleared the transom and quickly sank. The fiberglass engine cover lay cracked and shattered where Paul had been sitting only seconds before.

Donna screamed as Paul sank out of sight. She looked at the empty surface of the water helplessly and screamed again. In the space where her new husband had just been, all she could see were the engine belts spinning through shattered fiberglass.

She looked to Glen for help and found him prone on the deck holding his head, which was spurting out rich, red blood. He'd been hit by the engine cover as it flew off. He used his hand to try and staunch the bleeding as he stood up.

"Where's Paul?" Donna screamed.

"Down there, somewhere." Glen pointed into the depthless blue Pacific.

"We need to do something!" She now wished fervently that they had stayed in Tahiti, bored but safe at their seaside resort.

Glen stared into the ocean, thinking of the options. Paul was attached to the marlin by his rod, which was firmly secured to his chest harness. The fish was also attached to the chair. Glen could not remember if Paul had the seat belt on or not. He reasoned that Paul could be 1,000 feet away and 100 feet under. Jumping in after him would be useless. The best thing to do, he figured, was to look for anything floating to the surface: a hat, a cushion, maybe even Paul himself, and then take the boat there immediately. Glen looked around in every direction, all the way to the horizon. A full sixty seconds ticked by, moment by moment. And then another sixty seconds ticked by. In this time the marlin could have swum a long way and Paul's breath would surely have expired.

As Paul entered the water, time slowed way down for him. He felt the sensation of unbelievable pressure as the marlin pulled him along at great speed. A licensed dive master, Paul could not equalize quickly enough to keep his ear drums from puncturing. As he was being pulled under with no real chance of saving himself, he thought about all the bush plane trips he had piloted in Alaska, all the mountains he had climbed, and how crazy it was that a fish was now killing him. He knew he was going to die and the events of his life passed quickly before him.

Then, suddenly, he got angry and went into fight mode. Time sped back up as he began wrestling with his harness, forcing one arm through the loop despite the intense water flow against him. Then he got the other arm through and released himself from the harness, the rod, and the fish.

Maybe I can survive, he thought. He was an experienced free diver, who often went a hundred feet down in snorkel gear and stayed under for sixty seconds on a single breath. He began stroking straight up madly. But he had no idea that he was 200 feet deep. As he stroked and stroked without the surface getting near, he realized that the fish had not run, it had sounded. He concentrated all of his efforts to fight off unconsciousness. After swimming for a long, long time up through cold, dark water, Paul saw the hull of the boat. But he still had more swimming to do, and he knew from his dive training that he would most likely suffer a shallow-water blackout and not make it to the surface alive.

Most free-dive drownings happen when divers black out underwater, sometimes at the end of a long breath hold, but sometimes comfortably in the middle of a holding a breath. Unconsciousness typically strikes within 15 feet of the surface, where expanding, oxygen-hungry lungs begin to suck oxygen from the blood stream. The blackout happens quickly. The diver will not see tingle bells or feel light-headed. They have no sensation that it's coming. Paul had made it so close to the surface, and still he knew he might black out with no chance of avoiding death.

Glen and Donna heard a thunking sound on the side of the boat. They looked down to see Paul banging his fist on the hull. Donna's eyes poured out tears. Paul was conscious but panicked. He hit the surface and gasped down deep breaths in disbelief that he was still alive. "Praise God, I'm alive," he screamed.

Donna pulled Paul aboard. On his first try up the swim step, Paul fell right back into the ocean. The water in his inner ears had ruined his balance.

With Paul finally on board, Donna raced the *Karma* back to Kona, radioing the Coast Guard to have an ambulance waiting for the two injured men.

On the ride back Paul felt over and over again the sensation of rushing from the warm bright surface, through water that grew darker and colder. He felt the intense pressure in his ears despite the rapid-fire equilibrium adjustment that years of diving had made second nature for him. Then he felt the harness somehow release.

At the hospital, Paul was in better shape than Glen. A doctor drained water from his ears, then tested his lungs for inhaled water. Glen required numerous stitches for his head wound, and an x-ray revealed several broken ribs.

Within a few days, Paul was anxious to understand the mechanism of his survival. He asked Glen to take him out in the boat so he could dive the scene of the accident. He wanted to know how deep he had been carried by the marlin. Glen and Donna not only dismissed Paul's request, Glen emphatically said, "No!" and was quick to remind Paul that his boat was in need of repair, and he had no engine cover.

Undeterred, Paul rented a boat and scuba gear the next day from Jack's Diving Locker and went back out onto the blue seas. He took a wide open stride off the deck and plunged into the blue water. He sank slowly down to where he thought he had Houdinied out of the harness, the depth where he defied death. Then he took his mask off and slowly swam upwards. He estimated that the marlin had taken him down almost 200 feet below the surface before he reversed the descent. As he swam up without his mask he stopped when he could first make out the hull of the boat. His depth gauge read 30 feet. In this way he judged his depth during the incident and came to the conclusion that his survival was a miracle, not a feat of his own power.

A few days later, the newlyweds dined at a romantic restaurant in Kona, seated under a world-record blue marlin mounted on the wall. Paul looked up at the fish, and—suddenly and spontaneously—the rest of the sea-water drained out of his ear.

The accident didn't spook Paul. He still fishes and dives, when he's not flying planes in Alaska. But now he puts a little less faith in his skills and preparation and a little more faith in, well, faith. And he reminds himself that it's not often that the marlin releases the fisherman.

The Fish Garden

JOHN STRULOEFF

The drizzle was steady, a clinging mist like perspiration on my hands and face, feeding from the surf that struck the rocks. It was December. I was half a mile out on the South Jetty, which stretches in a narrow line of cold, gray boulders a mile or more between the Pacific and the churning mouth of the Columbia River. Every few seconds a wave would roll along the Pacific side and burst into a spray high above my head before continuing on. The wind was strong, carrying a cold mist that grated like ice across my face. I stood awkwardly on the rocks with a fishing pole in my hands, shaking, peering into the Columbia. The water there was gray and choppy, without the roll of the ocean. Faint in the mist were the dark mountains of Astoria. On both sides the water stretched unbelievable distances. I looked back to the line of jetty rocks curving to the beachhead where waves rolled like mighty hills.

My line was taut, anchored, it seemed, to the bottom of the ocean. I squeezed the cork handle of my pole. Out at sea a ship called in an echoing bass voice. Visibility was getting worse, less than a mile into the gray gloom.

It struck me again how vast the ocean was—even with the fog I could sense its magnitude. My brother had flown to Dutch Harbor the week before to go long-lining off the Aleutians, a few thousand miles straight out from where I sat, something he did every year after Christmas until early March. The job was dangerous, with high, frigid seas that dwarfed the waves along the jetty. I imagined him leaning low over the side into a mist, gripping the next 3-yard leader and pulling the great orange bulk of a halibut over the side, straightening his back tight before the slippery weight thudded onto the deck and slid to another man who guided it onto a conveyor, breathing through the frozen hairs of his beard as the winch coiled the longline up another 3 yards and he had to lean to grip the next leader. I've seen his pictures: workers like Titans in a rolling, frozen sea.

My father had raised me fishing, too, but I had married and stopped after high school. I had tried to make a new home away from the sea in the mountains with my wife. My father and brother were always much better fishermen—they had earned it with decades of their lives; somehow it had become art for them. For me, it had always been strangeness.

Before long, the words of an old sailor's song came to mind, and I sang, "Farewell and adieu to you fair Spanish ladies . . . Farewell and adieu to you ladies of Spain." I laughed and coughed onto my chest. "Farewell and adieu . . ."

A shock went through my pole.

The tip started downward, and I sat forward. Then the tip dropped. Line whizzed from the reel.

"Holy Christ," I said. The drag was set tight to slow the line, something I'd learned from fishing salmon. But it kept pulling. Not hard like a salmon or steelhead, but determined and heavy, like a sturgeon. I tightened the drag as far as it would go and grabbed my scaling-knife in case I had to cut the line.

The reel slowed to a stop. After a moment the line went slack, then eased tight and moved from my right across to my left in a long, slow circle, keeping the line snug.

"What's this?" I said. I was beginning the fisher's monologue—talking to his catch, a forced calm in his voice like he's talking down a gunman or a child on the verge of dropping an ancient vase. I stood and felt out a footing on the rocks, excitement and calm mixing in my blood.

The resistance kept up, with little tremors. I reeled slowly. You keep it steady, they won't feel it.

After maybe ten minutes of play, I still had no idea what was on the line. That was one of the excitements I remembered from fishing the jetty with my father—the absolute mystery, the feeling of something unknown but strong and alive guiding your line. In the rivers and streams there's finite variety—in the ocean, it's up to God.

Then it surfaced.

It rose slowly to just a few inches from the surface, enough so I could see a long black shadow, perhaps 3-and-a-half feet long. The head was huge and round, oversized for the body like a tadpole's. It rode the swell of a wave in front of me, bumping a rock. I stepped down to a smaller rock so my boots were close to the next wave's rise, reeling until a yard of line was between the tip of the pole and its mouth. It was a fish, certainly—inky, black, and amorphous in the water. Its front fins flapped slowly, its direction steady, body looking heavy and strong, resting.

A wave crashed, sending a bitter mist across my face and slopping water up my thighs. I set my feet and leaned back to heave my weight against the fish's, trying to hoist it out of the water. The head broke the surface, large as a bowling ball, and I could make out nubs—what should have been eyes—bulbous and black, reflecting the sky with a glossy sheen. It seemed to stare at me, though there were no eyes.

I leaned back further, and the mouth emerged, gaping wide with a sheer black depth, wide enough that my own head could have fit inside it. The hook was embedded in the thick flesh of its upper lip, and with the new pressure the body was about halfway out of the water. The pole bowed so sharply I thought it'd snap if I lifted it any further—a good hundred pounds. I eased the fish back into the water, and it opened its mouth once, its gills expanding.

My breath clouded in front of me, and I looked down the long stretch of rocks to the shore. "Christ," I said, then turned back to face what I had just caught.

Halfway back to shore, my hand cramped, so I found a flat rock and eased myself down. My shoulder hurt from leading the fish. It had been amazingly patient, even puffing its gills and flicking its tail to help.

"Farewell and adieu to you big bug-eyed bastard," I sang softly. I supposed then it still wasn't finished. I hadn't won yet. Not when the fish was still in the water.

"Alrighty," I said, conceding that much, and switched the pole to my other hand to flex my fingers. I lay the back of my hand against my cheek: cold as the sea.

When I was a few hundred yards from shore, the pain was agonizing, and I stopped to switch hands, flex, stretch my back and shoulders. The fish seemed to get impatient, moving in little circles, stopping to face away from the shore and flutter its front fins.

Then, with a rush of the tail, it made a run. The line whirred from the reel, and I dropped the tackle box onto the rocks. The box hit with a crack, and my hand cramped. I held with just my left hand, flexing my right as best I could, watching the reel spin. I breathed onto my hand and stuffed it in my pocket, flexing my fingers. I couldn't reel, so I watched the line draw further and further. It stopped weaving in the water and was on a straight line towards the deep. I felt dread watching the line go.

After a time, it began to hesitate, then slow—and as the line thinned on the reel and I could see the white plastic of the spool, it stopped. I slid my left hand up to grasp the line firmly against the pole. My heart pounded and shook my hands. The fish was tired—a second run is deathly exhausting.

I reeled quickly, holding the handle against my palm instead of up high between the knuckles of my thumb and first two fingers. I reeled until my hand cramped with a sudden and terrible burn. I pulled the line tight against the pole with my left hand and put my right in my pocket. I did this until the pain stopped at a sustained ache, and I was able to keep reeling.

The black liquid body rose, its head surfacing for just a moment. It began to lunge, but then its body was limp and went with the sway of the water. I stretched the pole to the side and pulled in some of the slack line to twist a loop-knot behind the second eye on the pole, to keep the fish from making another run.

I sat back, exhausted. The waves rolled with the wind, shooting up like geysers. What was I doing? All the pain and numbness, the damage I was doing my tendons and muscles and the cracking skin on my hands that would take days to begin feeling normal. Maybe for native whalers centuries ago, but for me?

I had a refrigerator full of food. A wife who was surely sitting on the couch in the warmth of central heating, sipping hot coffee, reading a book under a lamp while the wind blew outside through crackling firs and alders and across the frozen ground of our new land. I had a house with electricity and a new roof. I had a car and a job, a family and a savings account, a computer.

As I stood over the sand, I looked back along the jetty to where I had hooked the fish. My back ached, and I stretched, breathing hard. It had taken at least an hour. Exhilaration filled my body, and I whooped at the gray clouds. I felt I had done something very great. I had conquered. I imagined my brother working on his boat in the sweeping winds and high seas. We were a family of fishermen.

I hopped down onto the soft sand, and the wind nearly vanished, the roar easing to a breeze. A wave receded, and the black gleaming dome of the fish's head became exposed as the water eddied around and past it, leaving a line of thick yellowish foam where the water had reached furthest. The fish's gills widened the back of the head, then retracted. When the next wave began to peak, the fish was fully exposed on the sand. It was a huge fish, somewhat flattened now that it was out of the water, so that the first part of the belly behind the head was now wider than the head. The gills worked once, slowly. The way the nubs were arranged, on the top of the head and towards the front, bulbous and glistening, the fish seemed to stare, its large, soft mouth open.

The wave curled into a crash, and as the foam tumbled forward and started its long reach across the sand, I dug my heels in and pulled the fish away from the water so it couldn't turn back to the sea. I stopped at the water mark from the last high tide, where the foam dried in a white flaky line, small sticks strewn densely far down the beach.

The wind picked up, and the fish began collecting a thin coating, its inky skin losing its sheen and turning a mottled dark green. I stooped and looked closely. Its lower lip pulsed. The gills had gone still.

"I guess you're about done," I said, reaching out and touching a smooth patch of skin between the nubs. It was sticky, springy like gelatin. When I pulled my finger back, it had a grimy coating of sand that I wiped off on my pant-leg. I watched the nubs to see if they moved or opened into eyes, but they didn't. They were black and motionless. I looked at the fish for a time, and as I hoisted it into my arms, I remembered how difficult it is holding your kill in your hands.

The fish took up the whole back seat of my car. It slid like a snake out of my hands and fell onto the seat, making the car rock. As I lay my tackle box on the front seat, I saw a large crack in its corner and some of my lures and all of my weights were gone. With a sigh, I took the driver's seat and shut the door. A warmth moved across my body, and there was a hum in the quiet where my ears had lost the constant rush of wind and roar of waves. The wind belted the passenger side windows, but it seemed distant, a memory. My dashboard clock blinked the time: 9:37 a.m. I lay my head back and closed my eyes, listening to my breathing for a time before reaching for my keys.

The car warmed with the vents wide open. Something smelled thick and fetid, like from the bottom of a mud flat. I thought it was the worms, the dank way worms and earth will smell when mixed. Then I heard a long, draining gurgle and knew it was my friend on the back seat. I leaned forward to look into the rearview mirror, and I caught the black tip of a dorsal fin. Who knew where that thing had spent its years? Anywhere where the seas connect, anywhere in the great open.

The grass rolled in dark green and gold waves as I followed the beachhead out of the parking lot and onto the main exit-road of the park. Ahead were the dark slopes of the Coastal Mountains, and I soon passed the boat towns of Hammond and Warrenton, curving through the streets and climbing arched bridges above gillnet boats idling in the haze of exhaust and fog. I took a left onto Highway 101 and spanned the Youngs Bay bridge to Astoria, the jetty far across the bay where the river, bay, and ocean all mix waters. Here the mist thinned, and the mountains loomed across the river. The tops of the mountains could not be seen for the mist and clouds. Everywhere the world was wet and dark.

My parents' house was a faded burgundy ranch-style. It stood in a clearing walled with firs and maples, all darkened with winter's coloring. The house was fronted by thick rhododendrons as high as the eaves, much larger than my wife's. Father was surprised to see me. He opened the door in his robe and looked at me. His eyes were large and wide in his reading glasses. I hadn't seen him in weeks, not since my brother had left for Alaska. He seemed to have thinned some again, and his hair was a little disheveled, as if he'd been napping.

"Well, hello," he said, stepping back. "Come on in."

I had my hands deep in my pants pockets, and I tilted my head toward the car. "I caught something out at the jetty. Thought you might want to see." I was nervous for him to see the fish, and my voice shook a little

"Oh?" he said, his face relaxing into a smile.

"Mom around?" I asked, looking behind him to the darkened living room. The pictures on the walls glittered with flashes from the television. In high school she would take pictures of my brother and me with our catch, sending copies to relatives along with our school photos.

"In the restroom," he said. His voice was hoarse and quiet.

I turned and walked slowly back toward the car. He stepped out and closed the door. His slippers skated across the cement behind me.

"I used the treble-hooks you gave me for Christmas," I told him as I opened the door.

He stood beside me and stooped forward, giving me an expressionless look before peering into the dark cab.

"Good God," he said, adjusting his glasses up his nose. "What in the hell did you catch?" He looked at me with a strange, startled expression.

"I have no idea," I said. The fish had slid across the seat, its wide head mashed against the armrest on the far door. It looked utterly grotesque now to me, and my face grew warm with embarrassment.

He held the tailfin in his hand. The fin had collapsed together like an old Japanese fan and pointed straight back. He spread it wide and looked at it for a moment, then gripped the tail firmly and slid the whole body toward him.

"What is this thing?" he asked in a whisper, the way he used to do to his wood when he was working out a bad groove. "A bullhead?" He smacked the fish's back, and it wobbled. "Jesus Christ."

He leaned back, pushing his hands into the front pockets of his robe. He looked at the fish, then spit on the gravel. "You going to eat that thing?"

"I don't know."

He nodded and sniffed once. I could see in his withdrawn expression that he didn't understand why I had kept a fish I couldn't identify.

The front door opened, and my mother stepped out onto the stoop and put her glasses on. "Oh, hi," she said, smiling. "I thought that was your car."

I smiled for her and nodded. "Caught a fish out at the jetty—just showing Dad."

She closed the door softly and hurried to where we were standing. She put an arm around me, hugging me tight for a second, then stepped forward to look into the car. "Wow," she said. "That's some fish. Never seen one of those before. Kind of like the bullheads I used to catch when I was a kid."

Father cleared his throat. "You ever catch a bullhead that size before?"

Mom laughed. "Oh, well . . ."

Father spit again, then looked up into the fir trees at the edge of his property.

I suddenly recalled how long the fish had been out of water. I moved toward the driver's door. "Geez, I should get going. Got to get it put away if I'm going to do anything with it."

My mother shut the car door. Then she snapped her fingers. "Oh! I should get my camera."

I looked at the black mound in the back seat, and it gave me an odd, sick feeling in my stomach. "That's okay." I opened the door and sat down.

Father moved closer, his hands still in his pockets.

"Thanks for stopping by," Mother said. "That's quite the fish." She laughed as if we'd been sharing a story about high seas adventure.

I shut the door and rolled the window down. "Well, I should get this thing put away." I started the car.

My father leaned his head toward the fish. "You planning on eating that?" He still didn't understand what I was trying to do. And by then, neither did I.

"I don't know," I said.

I backed away. My mother waved, smiling wide and putting her arm around Father who stood, his hands in his pockets, as I drove beneath the dripping maples and onto the slick, dark road.

I pulled around the side of the house and into the grass. My wife came to the kitchen window wearing her glasses, and when she saw me she smiled and waved, then hurried to the sliding glass door and opened it. She was wearing a gray sweatshirt and jeans. She had never known me to fish.

"Catch anything?"

"Not really," I said.

I opened the back door, grabbed the fish by the tail, and heaved it out. It hit the ground with a squishy thump.

"My god," she said from behind me. I turned, and she was walking up slowly, her arms crossed over her stomach, her hands holding her elbows.

I dropped the fish's tail, and the rest of the body flopped into the grass.

"You caught that?" She moved her head slowly back and forth. "That is the biggest fish I've ever seen." She looked up to me, her eyes bright.

I put my arm around her, smiling for her like I had my mother. But it wasn't right. The fish wasn't right.

She smiled wide and hugged me close. "You're my fisherman."

She was beautiful to me then, with her awe of me she sometimes shows, her tenderness. But those feelings only saddened me because I knew she didn't know how hard it was to be a fisherman amongst the men in my family. The fish was just a dead thing to her.

We stood for a time and stared at it. Its mouth was open, fat lips grayish black, limp. The breeze picked up, cold and moist like at the ocean. She shivered against my side and pulled away, crossing her arms tightly against her chest. Then she leaned up and kissed my cheek softly before going inside, a tender smile still on her lips.

On the wind I could smell the ancient dankness of the fish, and then I knew where it belonged—a place where I'd seen my father bury hundreds of carcasses.

With a groan, my shoulders aching, I grabbed the fish's tail and began dragging the body to the soft soil of our garden.

Crash Course

MIKE LOVELL (WITH DAVE HURTEAU)

Temperatures had only climbed into the fifties by mid-afternoon on July 1, and the wind carried mist across the parking lot of the state boat launch in Hampton Harbor, New Hampshire. Despite the conditions, my friend Paul Johnson and I tossed our striper gear into his 16-foot tin boat and headed out. We figured a little stormy weather wouldn't kill us.

Right off the launch, I started catching schoolies and the sky began to clear—both good signs. Paul bragged about how pleased he was with his brand-new swivel seat; he kept swinging it around and adjusting its height. Both of us had flexible schedules—Paul is a painting contractor and I teach Theater Arts—but I think we may have taken off work to go fishing that day just so Paul could test out his fancy new boat seat.

We motored out to the Hampton River Bridge. Stretching from Seabrook Beach to Hampton Beach, the bridge spans the quarter-mile-wide mouth of Hampton Harbor, which opens into the Atlantic. There, we made the first of several drifts on an incoming tide. With a smallmouth rig and 8-pound test, I was tossing a big yellow bucktail with a pork-rind trailer and jigging it back across the current—and I was nailing fish.

What I couldn't seem to do, however, was land any of them—and I was in no small hurry to do so before my buddy did. I finally got a solid hook-up and played a big fish for a long time, until it raked the line across the underside of the boat and broke it. I switched to a big salt-water rig with 20-pound test and was just cinching down the knot on my jig when Paul pointed over my right shoulder.

"What's this asshole doing?" he said, peering past me. "He's heading right toward us."

About 100 yards off, a 45-foot fishing trawler was moving toward us. I shrugged it off and said, "Whatever. I'm fishing."

"I'm telling you," Paul insisted. "He's coming right for us."

I looked up again and was a little stunned at what I thought was a captain's arrogance in passing by a stationary fishing vessel on a course that would bring him within 30 feet of our boat. But I still didn't stop fishing. I was sure the captain could see us.

Finally, with the trawler only 40 yards away and Paul yelling, "He's coming right down on us!" I dropped my rod into the boat and assessed the situation. The big boat bore down on us at full throttle, but given its course, I could see it wasn't actually going to hit us. It would, however, throw a huge wake our way. So I set my feet for what I imagined would be a wild but probably harmless ride—a little like surfing.

Meanwhile, Paul was wisely scrambling to get us out of there. He punched the throttle of our idling outboard, but to his horror it only squealed for quarter of a second and died.

He grabbed the starter rope and pulled as the trawler notched over a little to its port side—that is, a little more toward us. Paul dropped the rope, stood up and began waving his arms and yelling. I quickly joined in.

While both of us screamed hysterically, I was watching the hull of the trawler. Even given the new angle, I still wasn't totally convinced it would connect with our boat. But then the whole scene changed. At just 20 yards, the trawler notched again to the port side, and the immense white bow turned to face us dead-on. It blocked out everything else. Suddenly, there was only this towering wall of steel and two hard facts: He doesn't see us. He's going to hit us.

I jumped out of our boat and barely cleared the gunwale when the bow of the trawler smashed into my head and shoulders. Then the bow was like a wall coming down, forcing me underwater. I slid deeper and deeper down the side of the trawler's hull into a murky green darkness.

Completely disoriented, all I could think about was being chopped up in the trawler's propellers. I kept seeing a cinematic image of giant, whirling steel blades and me in the middle of them. I turned and propped my feet against what I guessed was the bottom of the fishing boat and pushed off hard. Swimming away from the boat, I told myself I would stay as deep as I could for as long as I could, until the props had passed overhead.

I stayed under until I thought my lungs would collapse—until even the thought of swimming back toward the surface headfirst into the props couldn't keep me down a second longer. When I popped up, the trawler was about 100 yards away. I expected to see my buddy and our boat nearby, but I didn't. I looked left and right, and there was absolutely nothing around me.

Then there's the thing with my sunglasses. I wish I could say that this experience brought out some sort of heroic survival instinct, and temporarily granted me superhuman strength and senses. Instead, it seemed to make my thoughts unclear and less rational than ever. For some reason, I felt that losing my expensive polarized sunglasses was the greatest tragedy of all. Now, so far away from the scene of the impact, I dug through the water looking for them. The craziest thing was, I found them almost right away—out there in the current where the harbor opened up to the ocean. Then, for some reason, I continued to clutch them up over my head as I swam for shore, as if their value was greater than that of my life.

I'm not a good swimmer. Though I fish often, I usually do so with my feet on dry land. But looking over at the shore, I was confident that even I could make it from here, and that the swim in would be the easy part of this ordeal.

My only stroke is the sidestroke, so I couldn't see my progress. I swam for a long while, hoping to cover most of the distance in one strong burst. I wore heavy foul-weather gear. The pockets of air that had first kept me buoyant now filled with water. And of course, one of my arms was fully engaged in keeping my sunglasses safe. I took a break, expecting to be within spitting distance of the shore.

When I rolled around to the front, my heart dropped. I was much further away than before. The current had pushed me a mile from where

I had been. I looked in the direction I was heading and saw only more water. There was nothing I could realistically swim for. My only option was to tread water and hope to be rescued. That was the most helpless feeling I've ever had, sitting there waiting for somebody else to come and rescue me. I envied my friend Paul, who I knew was a great swimmer, and who I figured had at least ended up with the boat.

I didn't know it at the time, but Paul was still with the boat. To be more precise, he was still strapped into his new swivel seat, hanging upside down, and his boat was pinned to the bow of the trawler as it forged onward unaware. The trawler's impact drove the 16-footer's port-side gunwale slightly underwater and bent it around the front of the ship's bow. The starboard gunwale shot skyward and there the boat remained stuck, held by water pressure as the trawler chugged forward at full speed. And right with it—pinned upside down with his feet in the air, the gunwale of his own boat pinching his shins like the bar on a mousetrap, his head barely above water, and his fingers gripping the new swivel seat—was Paul Johnson, screaming futilely to the ship's captain.

As though the captain was napping, the trawler was now speeding toward the rocks of the Hampton Beach breakwater. Attached to the bow was Paul, gasping for breath through froth and spray, and fearing that he would be ground up against the breakwater any moment. By this point, he was sure that the boat was without a pilot. Perhaps the captain had suffered a heart attack and collapsed. He imagined for a moment that it was a ghost ship piloted by a crew of skeletons. The rocks of the breakwater would be his death.

Proximity to the breakwater was actually what saved him. The Hampton Beach area is something of a tourist destination, and the breakwater is a hot spot where folks kick back and gaze out onto the ocean. On this early summer day, there were dozens of tourists there, and upon seeing a man pinned to the bow of a fishing trawler, some of them started jumping up and down and waving their arms in an effort to gain the attention of the boat's captain. Mercifully, the trawler throttled down. As it did, Paul's boat came unstuck and Paul slid out of his seat and into the water.

Paul swam away from the trawler and toward shore. He wasn't having an easy time of it. But then suddenly, his new swivel seat—the one he'd been raving about all day and had been sitting on all through the worst boat ride of his life—popped to the surface. He grabbed it and floated and caught his breath. By that time, weekenders were tearing off their shoes and T-shirts, jumping into the water to help Paul.

Once on land, Paul told them that there'd been another person on the boat with him. The crowd called out my name like a chorus, but I was too far away to hear.

I was at least a mile from shore now. I could see land and tried to swim for it, but it was pointless. The current had taken me well into the giant bay. I was beyond tired. I could barely tread water. I had been trying to save myself for over an hour, and now I had a sick, sinking feeling that this could be the end.

Then something appeared in the distance. There was no mistaking the trawler that had run over us, and it was moving closer on a zigzag course, obviously searching for something. I waved my arms and saw the boat take a line toward me. I was relieved, but completely spent. I had about 30 seconds of treading water left in my muscles. If the trawler hadn't pulled up beside me and thrown me a line, I would have died.

I was amazed that the same boat that rammed us—so clumsily it seemed—could be steered so precisely within inches of my body on one try. Some mates threw me a line with a loop in it, and I slipped it over my shoulder with the hand that wasn't carrying my sunglasses. Then I endured the awkward experience of being winched up and pulled onboard like the day's catch. I reached the deck and first tossed my sunglasses onboard. "These are my sunglasses," I told the mate. "Watch out for them."

Once I was aboard, the captain looked at me and said, "Hey, sorry. I never saw you."

No shit you didn't see us! I thought. But he obviously felt bad, and I didn't have the energy to make him feel worse. I was thrilled to be out of the water, and still not thinking straight. I didn't know what had happened to Paul, but I assumed he was fine and had already started fishing again.

When I reached the boat dock, the police and marine patrol were waiting. I saw Paul walking down from the breakwater. He had a dead serious expression.

"I thought I'd lost a best friend," he said and hugged me—for the first time ever.

I replied by holding up my sunglasses and saying, "For a minute, I thought I'd lost my sunglasses."

We both spoke to the Coast Guard. Then they took the captain away to chat in private. Standing on shore in wet clothes, the chill soon grew unbearable. We decided to go home.

Truth is, I don't think either of us were thinking too clearly because once we started the car we started laughing as though the event had been a big joke. We were laughing on the drive home even when Paul pulled up his pant legs, and we both gaped wide-eyed at a cluster of big purple bruises and a horrible dent across his shins.

We stopped in the emergency room, and even there, we couldn't stop laughing long enough to describe to the doctor what had happened. At a convenience store, we were too hysterical to explain things to the clerk, but she gave me a dry shirt for free anyway. What were we laughing about? I still wonder.

That evening, I went to bed. I closed my eyes and began dreaming of sliding down the side of the trawler's hull, down into that murky green darkness again. I could see the giant metal props whirling, and then I woke up in a sweat. I stared at the ceiling for hours. At two in the morning, the phone rang.

"You sleeping?" Paul asked.

"No," I answered.

"Me either." The laughter had been replaced by gravity, whether we liked it or not.

To this day, people tell me that we were lucky. I suppose they mean lucky to be alive. But if I had been lucky that day, I would have caught that first big fish that broke my line.

The Greatest Fishing Story Ever Told

SCOTT CARRIER

I was in my office, staring at the wall, when my editor called to say the magazine wanted to send me on the fishing trip of my dreams.

I knew right away it was a trick question, perhaps dangerous, an offer too good to turn down.

"Can I go anywhere?" I asked.

"Yeah, within reason," he said.

"With Uma Thurman?"

"She's married and she just had a baby. I don't think she's available."

"Fine," I said. "Then I'll go alone."

But where would I go?

Someplace wild and beautiful, of course. Someplace for the water. The Sea of Cortes. Prince William Sound. Patagonia. Wisdom, Montana. A cold lake in a glacial cirque. A river with huge boulders that you swim out to and deep pools filled with big, dark trout. Someplace where there would be no other fishermen.

The next day, as it happened, a friend came by to show me an article about how the Nature Conservancy was trying to establish a national park in the Great Rivers region of Yunnan Province in China. The article had a map of the region, an area bordering Tibet and Burma where four major rivers nearly converge and run parallel through a gap 70 miles wide before spreading out and emptying to all of southeast Asia. The rivers were the Yangtze, the Mekong, the Salween, and the Irrawaddy, and the shape they made on the map was like an hourglass. There was also a photograph showing the director of the Conservancy's project, Ed Norton, standing with a 20,000-foot mountain in the background. I looked at the mountain and looked at the map and said, "There, where the rivers almost come together, that's where I'll go fishing."

"Does the article say anything about fish?" my friend wondered.

"It says the region is known for its remoteness and biodiversity. There's probably carp in the main rivers, and I'd guess there are trout up higher in the tributaries, like in the west. They could have migrated up any of these rivers, the same way they migrated up the Missouri and the Colorado. The Chinese are now promoting the area as the actual location of the Shangri-la Valley from James Hilton's novel *Lost Horizon*."

"I saw the movie," he said. "It wasn't bad. But you should really check to see if there are fish."

So I did some research. The best thing I found, by far, was Joseph Rock's 1947 monograph *The Ancient Na-khi Kingdom of Southwest China*. Rock was a self-trained botanist who lived in northern Yunnan from 1922 to 1949, working as an explorer for the U.S. Department of Agriculture and the National Geographic Society. His book was a detailed cultural history of the area, but it also included many black-and-white photographs of the terrain and the people who lived there. There were pictures of rivers running through deep gorges separated by mountain ranges with peaks covered in ice and snow, and there were pictures of high valleys, some with large lakes. The text displayed a level of detail that made me think I was looking at the product of a great mind, but, unfortunately, Joseph Rock was no fisherman. In fact, I found only one mention of fish in 500 pages, in a caption below a photo of four people in a boat. It read: "The lake is alive with fish, some of them poisonous."

It wasn't much, but I was looking on the bright side. I e-mailed Ed Norton and asked him if he knew anything about the fishing in the area. His reply came a few days later: "There is no fishing in any of these rivers—no sport fishing, anyway." I wrote back, asking him to be more specific. After two weeks, when nothing had come back, I called Norton's office in China but was told he had left for the forest and wouldn't be back for a long time.

I wondered whether he had meant that there were no fish in the rivers or that catching them wasn't allowed or that people in China don't do "sport fishing." I wondered whether I was a sport fisherman. I'd never considered it a sport. For me, it didn't have anything to do with competition or rules. It was a way to carry my fly rod around and hang out next to water. But then the fly rod was a weapon, and that was why I liked to hold it.

In the end, the question of Norton's reply came down to the definition of sport, which I didn't really want to think about. I was going fishing, regardless of definition.

I flew into Kunming, the capital of Yunnan, a city of skyscrapers and three million people, and got on a bus going north, toward Tibet, toward the mountains where the rivers almost came together, the center of the hourglass. In a day's ride, I was in Lijiang, on the southern base of Jade Dragon Snow Mountain (elevation 18,150 feet). I got off the bus in the late afternoon, and there it was, like an entire range unto itself, rising up from out of nowhere, dwarfing the other mountains in the area. The air was cool and dry, and the light was sharp; it had the feel of the basin and range, a feeling of high, open space—a perfect place to fish.

The streets of Lijiang were wide and white, with stoplights that gave digital countdowns of the seconds remaining until the change to green. Everything was new, and the air smelled of fresh concrete. I'd read that Lijiang was hit by a huge earthquake in 1996 that leveled much of the communist architecture. In its place they seemed to be building hotels, hotels, and more hotels, all in a sort of a brutal fortress look but finished in white tile and done up with banners and flags like desert casinos. I went into one, but there was no one at the front desk who spoke English. I tried a couple more; same thing. They seemed uninterested in Western tourists.

I got in a cab and told the driver, "Hotel," but she didn't know what that meant, so I threw up my hands, and she took me to the old part of town, the part that was built eight hundred years ago and had withstood the earthquake and was being preserved as a living-history theme park.

This was where the Western tourists stayed—or maybe this was where we were put. The streets were narrow and mazelike and paved with large stones that had been worn smooth over the centuries. There were shops selling carved animals, jewelry, and Tibetan clothing, restaurants along a stream with outdoor seating under willow trees and the Eagles on the sound system, guesthouses with internet connections and signs in English, German, and French. It was a bustling place filled with tourists, only a few of whom were Westerners. The vast majority were middle-class Chinese, on vacation for the first time ever.

The next morning, I got in a cab and said, "*Wo yao diao yu*"—I'm looking for fish—a phrase that I'd learned from a Chinese student in a restaurant the night before. The driver nodded and drove north out of town, toward Jade Dragon Snow Mountain, and stopped after 12 to 15 miles at what looked like a retreat center a little ways up the southern slope. There were a series of large pools, one above another, up to a spring where the water came gushing out of the side of the mountain. There were walkways around the pools with Chinese tourists strolling slowly, some arm in arm, dressed as though they were going to church. In the pools were trout, big trout, hundreds of them.

I hadn't flown halfway around the world to fish at a trout farm, but I was curious to see what kind they had here. So I asked a woman who worked there if it was okay for me to fish. She pointed to a pool, and I set up my rod, attracting some attention from other employees. My fly box was stained with blood, and opening it was like looking into a living organism, something that had heat and perspired—little killers, little pieces of meat made from silk and deer hair and feathers. I tied on a scud, which looked like a small shrimp—simple, irresistible. I threw out 30 feet of line, and there was an immediate boiling in the water as one fish took the hook and a hundred others swarmed over it, as if they were going to devour the thing before I could pull it to shore. It was a 4-pounder, shaped like a rainbow but with none of the color. It was dark-brown and black, with only a little white underneath and no distinct spots, and its fins and tail had been eaten down to nubs—not a pretty sight. I put it back and it swam away.

"This fish is dead," said the woman who worked there. "You pay me 200 yuan." Which was twenty-five dollars.

"It's not dead," I said. "It swam away just fine."

"This fish is dead. 100 yuan per kilo. You pay me 200 yuan."

She seemed quite sure of herself, and although I took umbrage, she would not back down. I decided to compromise and gave her half of the money and walked away wondering what had just happened. Twenty-five dollars for a fish in a country where the average annual income is 700 dollars? This seemed rather excessive. Maybe these were special fish, rare or somehow sacred. Or maybe I had been ripped off. There was no way to say for sure.

I walked down the mountain, following the stream through steep pastures and cornfields surrounded by rock walls. The corn was full-grown, and there were people harvesting, cutting the stalks by hand and loading them onto horse-drawn wagons. I would tell them that I was looking for fish, and they would smile and sometimes laugh. They seemed to have no problem with me coming out of nowhere with a fly rod and walking across their land. Back home I would have been shot for such behavior, but these people apparently had a different concept of private property. Perhaps they didn't mind because there were no fish in the stream to catch. The stream was clear and cold, but there were no plants growing in it. I turned over rocks, looking for bugs and nymphs. Nothing. I looked around in the bushes on the shore and saw a caterpillar. So I tied on a caterpillar fly, the same size and color, and threw it across the stream so that it landed under some bushes along the shore, as if it had fallen from one of the branches. I threw it just above the pools, letting it drift and sink. I threw it on top of a fallen log and let it roll off into the water. Nothing. I tried four or five other flies, dry and wet.

There was nothing living in the water.

That night, I had dinner beside the stream in Old Town. The air was a little cold—sweater weather—and it reminded me of Halloween. The willow tree over my head was turning yellow and dropping leaves in just the same way it would on Deer Creek in southern Utah. The other people sitting along the stream looked as if they were from all over the world, East and West, young and old, everyone listening to Joni Mitchell and enjoying the night.

I was working on my second beer when a young American introduced himself and asked if he could be of service. His name was Eric Mortensen, and he was a PhD candidate in Inner Asian and Altaic studies at Harvard. He'd been coming to the area for ten years to study raven divination among the shamanist hill tribes. He spoke Chinese and Tibetan and had read everything—absolutely everything—about the area. He said he had a topographic map, but he didn't want to take it out in public as topo maps were until recently considered state secrets, so we went into the restaurant and up to the second floor, where there were a couple of tables and a 20-watt bulb hanging from the ceiling. The map showed an area west of Lijiang, between the Yangtze and the Mekong.

"I've read that the distance between the four rivers is less than a hundred miles," I said. "Would it be possible to traverse the ranges and see all four?"

"You would die. Or maybe I should ask, How are your mountaineering skills?"

"Well, I'm not looking to get out on a glacier, but I think I could walk through some snow over a pass."

"It would take months," he said. "The area is huge. How much time do you have?"

"A couple weeks. I'm looking for fish."

"Well, I've seen big fish being caught in the Mekong near Laos. Maybe you should go down there."

"No, I'm interested in clear water and high elevation, although not any higher than, say, where a grasshopper would live."

"You should go to Haba," he said. "Haba Snow Mountain. It's just north of Jade Dragon Snow Mountain, with Tiger Leaping Gorge running in between. Haba village is on the eastern side of the mountain, at about twelve thousand feet. Up above the village, another 2,000 feet, is a small lake they call the Black Sea, and I saw people fishing there."

"Do you know what kind of fish are in the lake?"

"I don't know what they were catching."

"It could be trout," I said.

"Or it could be nothing," he said.

I was at the bus station by 7 a.m. Mortensen had told me how to get to Haba: Ride a bus north for a day to Zhongdian, ride another bus southeast for a day to Baishuitai, then walk south for a day to Haba. He'd said I could also get there through Tiger Leaping Gorge but that I should really go to Zhongdian just to see it and to visit the Songzanlin Monastery nearby.

"Before you go into the monastery," he'd said, "be sure to buy a *khata*, a white scarf. Then ask the monks to introduce you to the head lama. I think you'd enjoy talking to him. Give the *khata* to him, formally, by bowing your head as you put it around his neck. That way you'll show the proper respect." I didn't really know what I'd say to a head lama, but I had his name written in Tibetan in my notebook, and I thought that if I had some time I might stop by for some tea and a chat. The first order of business, however, was to get to Zhongdian.

The bus was old and dirty, with a 5-foot-high stack of cargo tied on top, and the inside was so packed with people and stuff that you had to crawl over rice sacks and boxes to get in or out. We sat at the station lined up with other buses that were being loaded, all of them idling. Behind the buses was a line of seven women in police uniforms, standing at attention. The air was foggy and thick with diesel exhaust and the stench of shit from the public toilet. The other men on the bus were either smoking or hacking up big globs of phlegm from deep inside their lungs—a violent rendering that was spat out the windows. Eventually, the driver got on board and sat down behind the wheel. He lit a cigarette, put a glove on his right hand, and began a long search through the gearbox for reverse. The bus crept backward and then stopped, as the driver told his assistant to run into the station and waste some more time so that the inside of the bus could fill up with exhaust and all the passengers would be comatose for the ride. It took a long time to get out of there, the seven women still standing at attention as we pulled away.

We followed the road up over a low saddle that was part of the southern flank of the Jade Dragon, then dropped 1,500 feet to the Yangtze River, which was a couple hundred yards wide, muddy, and flowing fast, boiling up and swirling in whirlpools that opened and closed without warning. The canyon topped out at a high pass that opened up to a long green valley with mountains in the distance, very much like places in Wyoming.

Zhongdian was a cloud of dust rising up off the prairie, and then it was a city under a cloud of dust, and then it was some dirt roads lined with stacks of old boards, disassembled engines, piles of rocks and sand and bricks, and little pigs wandering through the traffic of lizard-like tractors and three-wheeled moto-rickshaws, and then it was the center of a town with a monumental statue of a man racing a horse, running full speed. A street with single-story shops—dark coveys with galvanized buckets and yak-hair dust mops hanging out front, the House of Dog Meat Restaurant, CD kiosks—ran in a circle around the statue, and above the shops was a billboard, dwarfing everything but the statue, of a herd of yak bulls stampeding across a high plateau. It was a rip-off of a Marlboro ad, only the cigarettes were called Honghe. The pack looked just like a Marlboro pack, and yet something was missing. The billboard had the landscape and the bulls, but it did not have the man; there was Honghe Country, but there was no Honghe Man, which seemed like a mistake.

Zhongdian was much smaller than Lijiang, and higher, at eleven thousand feet. After we pulled in, I hopped off the bus and bought a map, one with "Welcome to the Land of Shangri-la" on the cover, and made my way to the Long Life Hotel, which catered to Western backpackers.

The next morning, I went to the bus station and tried to buy a ticket to Haba, but the woman at the counter said, "*Meiyou.*" I'd never heard the word, but it was clear what it meant: "It's not going to happen." I pulled out my map and could tell she understood where I wanted to go, but either the bus had left or there was no bus or there were no tickets or who knows; it just wasn't going to happen. *Meiyou.* So I decided to visit the Songzanlin Monastery, as Eric Mortensen had recommended.

It was 2 miles north of town, built into the side of a hill, like the Potala in Lhasa, only smaller and not in nearly as good shape, as it had been used for artillery practice by the Red army during the Cultural Revolution. I bought a white silk scarf at the gate and walked up 300 vertical feet of steps to the temple entrance. I was inside, looking at the statue of a golden Buddha, when they started to blow the big horns and all the monks came running in for a prayer meeting. They sat cross-legged on long, padded benches, the older monks up front close to the golden

Buddha, the young boys in the back by the door, where I was. The little monks quickly became bored and began goofing off. An 8-year-old had a plastic bag that was inflated and tied like a balloon, and he was batting it around in the air. The monk next to him, who was maybe ten, grabbed the balloon and bit a hole in it, and the younger kid picked it up and crammed it down the older kid's mouth, and the older kid acted as if that was okay because now he was a scary monster with a bag in his mouth. And so on, slugging and pushing. *Om mani padme hum.*

When the prayer was over, I went outside and sat in the courtyard. A young monk came over and pointed to my fly rod on the side of my pack, so I took it out and showed it to him. I put the rod together and got out the reel and line and had a little demonstration. Soon, there were thirty or forty other monks crowded around watching. I opened my fly box and felt all the heads bend forward, looking down at what was inside. I took a black fly I'd made years ago and tied it on and told everyone to give me some room. I tried to teach them the basics—not moving your arm past 10 and 2 o'clock, waiting for the line to straighten out in front and in back, using the flex of the rod to throw the line. Then I gave the rod to one of the monks, and he threw the line around, immediately snapping off the fly. Then he started whipping the other monks, who ran in all directions, laughing. Then they all took turns whipping and running away, while I was trying to get them to stop and learn how to do it correctly, saying, "Wait! Be careful! You'll put somebody's eye out!"

Finally, I put the rod away and asked one of the monks if I could talk to the head lama. I showed him my notebook where Eric Mortensen had written the man's name in Tibetan. He nodded and took me to the kitchen next to the temple. It was a dark room with a fire in an open pit on the floor, smoke going up three floors and out through a window on the roof. The walls were black with a soft shine. Two copper vats were on the fire—one with yak-butter tea, the other with yak stew. The cook motioned for me to sit down by the fire and poured me a cup of the tea. There were four or five other monks sitting around the fire, and they all watched to see if I would drink it. So I did. A little sip produced a pucker and a gag reflex that I squelched as best as possible. Boiled rancid butter is boiled rancid butter and not something you easily develop a taste for.

Afraid that the cook would want me to drink some more tea, I pulled out my minidisc recorder, microphone, and earphones and let the monks listen to themselves talking and laughing. This upset one of the older monks, and he told me to put the thing away, which I did. But then he left the room, and the monks begged me to take it out again, so I did, only to have the older monk come back and get even more upset. "Goodbye! Goodbye!" he yelled, pointing to the door. So I got kicked out of the monastery and never met the head lama, which was okay because I didn't know what to say to him anyway except "I'm looking for fish."

My "Land of Shangri-la" map showed that there was a lake not far from the monastery, so I got in a cab and pointed to the lake, and the driver took off. We went there, but the lake was dry—or, rather, it had receded to about a mile from where the road ended. I grabbed my rod and walked in the direction of the water until the ground became too muddy. The sun was going down behind the mountains, and some big white birds were flying up into the sunlight and then circling back down to the marsh. I took out my binoculars and saw they were black-necked cranes, with long legs and 6-foot wingspans, standing 5 feet tall in the mud. I could see them looking back at me, and it took my breath away. They were not fish, but they were wild and beautiful, and so they counted.

I got an early start the next morning, heading out for the bus station before the sun had come up, the streets empty except for a few moto-rickshaw drivers wearing long coats and fur hats to cut the cold wind. None of them had passengers, but that didn't stop them from cruising about, perhaps for the heat coming off the engines. Just before the bus station, there was an open-air market, and I went inside and saw big carp for sale. Some were dead, in a basket, and others were alive, swimming around in a wooden box lined with plastic. I asked the guy where they came from, and he said, "Bita Hai." Bita Lake was only 25 kilometers west of Zhongdian, on the way to Haba.

I bought a bus ticket to the Bita Hai Nature Preserve, where I was given a pamphlet. "Among the Shangri-la snow area, Bita Hai is the most beautiful lake that is surrounded by primeval forest at 3,540 meters above the sea level," it read. "The 'Zhongdian double-lip fish' is the only of its kind which is still living on the globe. In spring, when the azaleas are in full bloom, the fishes will eat off the petals dropped from the azaleas and become 'drunk' and lie on the surface of the lake...."

I was walking from the entrance when an SUV stopped to give me a ride. There were two young Chinese women in the back, dressed for a business lunch in Beijing. They said they worked for the China International Travel Service and had just flown into Zhongdian that morning for a tour of the area.

"Where are you going?" one of them asked.

"To the lake."

"You can call me Shirley," she said, "and this is my friend Lisa."

The driver stopped in a parking lot, where a trail led down through a pine forest to the lake.

"Most people take horses from here," Shirley said, "but my friend and I will walk. Would you like to come with us?"

"Sure," I said, although I quickly regretted it. Shirley and Lisa were wearing high heels, and while there was something strangely appealing in watching their ankles shake and quiver, they couldn't cover much ground. We were passed by long lines of horses carrying other tourists down to the lake—the men in jackets and ties, the women in business suits and heels, the same as my new friends. They dressed up. They didn't go alone. And they littered a lot. It was a different way of meeting the wilderness.

Lisa wanted to rest, and she sat down on a fallen tree.

"We are at the number-one hotel in Zhongdian," Shirley said. "You can have dinner tonight with us?"

"Sure," I said. "I'd like that." But I was really thinking that these two had nothing to do with fishing, and I wanted to ditch them and get down to the lake.

"What is that?" Lisa asked, pointing to my fly rod.

"It's a fishing rod. I'm going try to catch a fish in the lake."

"There is no fishing here," said Shirley. "It is not allowed."

"Because of the two-lipped fish? They're trying to protect it?"

"I don't know the two-lip fish, but there is no fishing here."

"Tonight you have our fish soup at hotel," Lisa said.

"That's a nice offer," I said, but it wasn't really what I had in mind. I was upset. The guy in the market had been pulling my leg.

That night I sat alone in the restaurant at the Long Life Hotel, back in Zhongdian, listening to Karen Carpenter sing that song about her favorite song. The walls of the cafe were lined with Tibetan *tangka* paintings of *bodhisattvas* floating on lotus blossoms and three-eyed *herukas*, evil demons, with headdresses of skulls and flames standing on dismembered bodies of tormented souls. The waiter asked me if I liked the music and I lied, saying yes, so he played it over and over and I had to tough it out. Sometimes, I thought, a fisherman needs to be patient. Sitting and waiting was the first thing I'd learned about fishing, from sitting with my grandfather in a boat on the Lake of the Ozarks, not saying a word or catching a fish for an entire morning. Sometimes you just have to sit there and do nothing.

I woke up feeling anxious and full of self-doubt. I had been in China for one week and I had not found the fish I had come for, and, worse, I seemed to have lost the ability to predict the consequences of my actions. Each morning, I had set off with a plan, and each day I had seen the plan unravel, and each night I ended up eating alone in the restaurant, listening to the Greatest Pop Hits of All Time. Something was wrong, and I decided to spend the day thinking about what it might be.

Perhaps, I thought, Haba is not the place to go. My original goal was to go where the rivers came together, the center of the hourglass. I looked at my map. Zhongdian was close to the center of the hourglass, but the next town north, Deqin, was even closer. Deqin was between the Yangtze and the Mekong, at 14,000 feet above sea level. The highest peak in Yunnan Province, at 22,000 feet, was 20 miles west of town. This seemed like the place to go.

So with a new resolve, I got on a bus headed for Deqin. We drove uphill for four hours and topped out at a 15,000-foot pass. At that point, the driver stopped, and everybody got out and lay down on the tundra grass to try to hide from the wind, which was blowing 40 miles an hour and cold like winter. Just below the pass was a larch forest, turning orange. Beyond, looking west, was a massive ravine, twice the scale of the Grand Canyon. At the bottom was the Mekong River, which emptied at Saigon. On the other side of the canyon was the Kha-wa-kar-po mountain range, with glaciers hanging from the jagged peaks more than 20,000 feet high. Beyond the Kha-wa-kar-po was another canyon with the Salween River, which emptied in southern Burma. Turning around, I looked back at the mountains to the east where everything drained into the Yangtze, which ended at Shanghai. I closed my eyes and tried to imagine all of southeast Asia, but I couldn't. I tried to imagine the Tibetan plateau to the north, where all the rivers began. Water. The crashing of continental plates. It was all too much. I stood up, surrounded by my fellow passengers, and with outstretched fly rod scanning the horizon said, "I hereby claim these rivers and the land they drain as the rightful property of God and the king of Spain." My small audience was silent for a second and then burst into laughter—the only appropriate response.

From the pass, the road ran north along the eastern slope of the canyon. The terrain was steep in every direction, and I realized that there would be no rivers or lakes to fish here, only waterfalls. The town of Deqin was built in a long, steep gully, like an avalanche chute, so I decided to keep going and try to find someplace with level ground. There were three roads heading out of town. One ran north along the Mekong into Tibet, but this was not an option, as I didn't have the proper visa and there would be a guard station at the border. Another ran south along the Mekong, but this was closed due to a landslide. Which meant I'd have to wait and go back the way I'd come, to Zhongdian, in the morning.

It rained off and on through the night, and at sunrise I could smell snow. Deqin had just been dusted, but there were 8 inches going back over the pass. I was lucky to get out at all.

I spent the evening next to the wood-burning stove in the cafe at the Long Life Hotel, listening to Karen Carpenter sing that song about her favorite song, wondering if I had fallen into a twilight zone. Perhaps my plane had crashed over the Pacific and I was dead. Or perhaps I was just fucking up in a major way here. Either way, the *herukas* on the wall seemed ready to pounce.

Then, as if on cue, a Tibetan man, about 35, walked into the cafe and sat down next to me. He was short, with long hair that hadn't been washed in a while and a face that broke into thirty pieces when he smiled. It was the smile of a man who'd spent a long time in the mountains. He was wearing a large windbreaker, but his left sleeve was pulled up, and I could see that his arm was shrunken, his hand mangled and upside down.

"Where do you come from?" he asked me in good English.

"Utah, in America."

"Arches?"

"Yes," I said. "Exactly."

"I saw photos. Very beautiful."

His name was Xia Shanquan, but he went by Sean. He was a guide and owned a guesthouse in Tiger Leaping Gorge. He'd come to Zhong-dian for a meeting about tourism but was going back home in the morning. I told him I was trying to get to Haba, and he said I could go with him to his house in the gorge, which was only a day's walk from Haba.

"Are there fish near Haba?" I asked him.

"There are fish in the Yangtze. People catch them with dynamite," he said, laughing so hard he almost fell over in his chair.

"But how about up on the mountain, in the lake called the Black Sea?"

"I think maybe there are snow fish in the lake. People catch them with insects."

"Grasshoppers?"

"I will show you. I don't know the name in English."

I couldn't believe my good fortune.

Tiger Leaping Gorge had the shape of a very narrow and deep V. At the top of the V were two peaks, Haba Snow Mountain (16,000 feet) and Jade Dragon Snow Mountain (18,000 feet), and at the bottom was the Yangtze River (8,000 feet), which seemed to go out of its way, turning almost 180 degrees, to run between the mountains. The name Tiger Leaping Gorge came from the canyon being so narrow that a tiger was said to have once leapt across it.

Sean's guesthouse was 22 kilometers into the gorge along a road that had been cut into the wall of the canyon. We rode there in a toy-like pickup truck, Sean sitting up front in the cab with the driver and four other men. I sat in the bed with bags of rice and corn, 5-gallon cans of gasoline, and five other people. The road was muddy, as there had been three straight days of rain, and the truck's little engine struggled mightily, the rear wheels spinning and fishtailing. Sometimes we all got out to push and pull with a rope, sometimes we moved boulders that had fallen in the road, and sometimes we stood and watched while the driver crept between spaces just inches wider than the 4-foot wheelbase of the truck.

The road had been slowly gaining elevation above the river, so looking down at it produced an instant rush of vertigo. The river was monstrous, exploding through canyon walls that were only 25 yards apart. I'd never seen anything so powerful, and it yanked hard on my heart. I could not see the edge of the road because we were so close to it. I could hear a stream of water running under the truck, and I could hear a stream of water falling on top of the truck, and there was no road that I could see. If the truck were to slide over the edge, the fall line would start as a series of tumbles and pirouettes—a flinging of bodies and bags of rice—and end in the crashing of water that would pound everyone and everything into miscellaneous bits of unrecognizable pulp and flattened metal.

I was deeply scared, but I was also happy, even overjoyed. It was wild and beautiful, and so it counted. It was what I'd come for.

After 20 kilometers, the truck stopped at a guesthouse and everybody got out. "My place is 2 kilometers from here," Sean said, "but the road is gone up ahead. We need to look at it."

We walked up the road, lifting fallen boulders out of the way. It was getting dark, hard to see, but up ahead there was no road. The side of the mountain had slid away. I wanted to get closer, but Sean stopped me. "You see, it's still dripping," he said, pointing to a patch of mud sliding down the slope. "Not good. It rains for three days and this is what happens."

"What do you want to do?" I asked.

"We can run across it, very quickly."

"Run?" I said. My pack weighed 50 pounds. It was almost dark. The slope was slippery and steep.

"Yes," he said. "Unless you want to stay here or ride back to town in the truck."

"I'll go," I said.

"Then follow me." And he took off running. It was a mad dash for 300 yards, some of which was out on the muddy slope, completely exposed, so that a slip would mean a long slide to some cliffs and then a longer fall to the river. I ran with my fly rod in my hand for balance, following Sean's steps as closely as possible. He ran fast, without stopping, and I thought I heard him laughing. And then I realized I was laughing. It seemed impossible to run across that slope in the dark, and yet it also seemed as if all I had to do was keep up with Sean and everything would be all right. It was like skiing right behind a friend. It was like following someone off a cliff. It was as much fun as I've ever had in my life.

We stopped at a waterfall where the road started again. I was saying something like "That-was-un-fucking-believable-you're-completely-out-of-your-mind-I've-never-done-anything—" when a boulder as big as a house came crashing down the slope and rolled across where we had just passed, launching itself into thin air and disappearing into the darkness before being smashed into a million pieces.

"You like this?" Sean asked.

"I love this," I said, and we both laughed and ran down the road toward his house.

Sean's guesthouse was two stories high, framed in post and beam, with big windows looking out over the canyon. Standing on the patio out in front, I could see four or five lights from other houses across the hillside. I could see the dark outline of the mountain on the other side of the canyon. I could hear the roar of the river 1,000 feet below.

We ate in the kitchen next to the wood stove. It was there where he told me what happened to his arm. He was born healthy in 1964, but when he was 2 and a half years old, during the Cultural Revolution, the Red army came looking for his father. His father wasn't home, so they grabbed Sean and threw him in the fire, and then they grabbed his sister and threw her off a cliff. Sean said it was not just his arm but the entire left side of his body that had been burned. "They called me 'flower pig' because my skin was like a flower pig—many colors," he said.

"There was no hospital?"

"There was no road, no bicycle, nothing. They would have had to carry me."

As a kid, he went to grade school, but the Communist party wouldn't allow handicapped kids in middle school or high school. So he educated himself.

When the communists allowed small-scale capitalism in the late eighties, Sean started the first store in the village. When they opened the area to tourism in 1993, he built the first guesthouse. He learned six languages.

"Do you hate the Chinese for what they did to you?" I asked.

"It's not a very good culture," he said. And then he smiled and his face broke up.

That night, before I went to sleep, I realized that in order to catch my flight out of Kunming in 5 days, I would have to walk all the way to the Black Sea lake and back to Sean's guesthouse in 2 days, which seemed like it might be impossible. Walnut Grove, where Sean lived, was on the south side of Haba Mountain, at about 9,000 feet. Haba village was on the east side of the mountain, at about 12,000 feet. The lake was 2,000 feet above the village. I would be able to do it only if I could see well enough to walk at night. I turned off the light in my room and looked out the window and saw nothing but black.

The next morning I told Sean that I was going to try to get to the lake and back in 2 days, and he said he didn't think I could do it.

"It's very far, and there is snow up high, around the lake."

"Snow is okay," I said. "A little bit, anyway." I told him I'd pay him to come as my guide, but he said he had clients who were flying into Zhongdian and he had to go back up there and meet them.

"Today," he said, "you can go to Haba. Tomorrow go to the lake. But, I'm thinking, maybe there are no snow fish now. They are very expensive, more than 80 yuan (10 dollars) per pound."

"You mean the lake has been fished out?"

"They take the film off the skin and sell it as medicine. It is a wild fish, so it is a medicine."

"All wild fish have medicinal value?"

"Yes, for the Chinese. So maybe there are no snow fish left."

That was kind of a letdown, but I still wanted to go to the lake. Sean gave me some directions to Haba that included a shortcut that would take three hours off an eight-hour walk. I said goodbye and thanks, and I left feeling sad that I'd never see him again.

At 4 p.m. I walked into Haba village along a path that wound through the terraced fields. The air smelled sweet, like expensive perfume, and then I realized it was from the marijuana plants, which were 7 feet tall and lined the edges of the fields. They had buds longer and thicker than my forearm, buds that sparkled with tiny beads of oil but were full of seeds. The plants were grown for their fiber.

There was a stream running through the village, fed, perhaps, by the lake up above. It was a stream that could easily have held trout, so I turned over some rocks and looked carefully for anything living, but there was nothing there—just clear, cold water running over orange and silver stones. Still, I sat down and put my rod together and tied on a grasshopper. I wanted to fish. I asked myself, what is the motive of the grasshopper? Why does it try to jump over the stream, only to fall into the water? Perhaps, I thought, it sees the reflection of the sky in the water and thinks it's jumping into thin air. What a surprise, then, when it hits the water, sort of stunned, and then struggles to fly away while being swept downstream. I made my grasshopper commit this mistake over and over again, putting it through many slow deaths, watching as it was swallowed by whirlpools and it tumbled over stones. An insect in peril is a tantalizing thing to a fish, and my grasshopper fly gave a fine performance.

Then I noticed there were others watching. There was an old woman not more than 20 feet away, standing motionless, staring at me. And two young boys, one on a bicycle, on the road. When they saw me, they started waving their arms and yelling at me, like maybe I shouldn't be fishing there. Fine, I thought, there are no fish in the stream anyway.

I walked on a bit farther and then took my pack off and sat down on a stack of logs. I pulled out my binoculars and looked up at the top of Haba Mountain, studying the slope for ways I could ski up and down, as if the opportunity might sometime arise. A man came walking along and stopped to watch me looking through the binoculars, so I let him look for a while, which he seemed to like a lot. I showed him my rod and flies and then asked him, in Chinese, if there were fish in the lake, pointing up the mountain. He shook his head—*meiyou*—and pointed down toward the Yangtze. I wanted to tell him I wasn't interested in fishing in muddy water, but I couldn't.

I checked into a guesthouse and sat in my room smoking a wet joint and pondering, once again, my situation. The room had one light bulb that stayed on for a minute and then went off for thirty seconds, and then came on for ten seconds and went off for three seconds, and then it was on for a minute. I had a choice: I could stay and go to the lake and miss my plane out of Kunming and worry about a new reservation later, or I could turn around in the morning and start back. It would take two days to get to Lijiang, and then at least another two days to get to the airport in Kunming. I'd been gone for more than two weeks, and back home my wife had been working days and nights, choreographing the dance scenes for *Oliver!*, the school play. I'd called her from Zhongdian, and she said things were fine but that she was tired and wanted to know if I would be back in time for opening night. "It's kind of important," she said. "We could all go together."

If I missed my plane, I'd miss the play. I'd finally made it to the place where I'd been trying to go, and perhaps the man with the binoculars had been wrong. Maybe there were snow fish in the Black Sea. It would take only about six hours to walk there and check it out. It was either this or leave in order to sit in a high school auditorium watching kids sing, in bad British accents, about the boy who asked for more. It seemed a cruel choice. Finally, the light went out and didn't come back on, and I fell asleep.

In the morning, I got up and went outside to look at the mountain. Storm clouds had come in and were hanging around the peak as though they wanted to live there for a while. I sat down on the stack of logs and decided I'd had a good trip and that it was time for me to go home. That way, I could take my time and not worry, time enough to get lost walking back and enjoy it. That way, the fish would never be caught. They would remain in my dreams—a lake high in the mountains, an inch of snow around the shore, little blue-and-yellow flowers poking up from the tundra grass, and a fish looking up at a grasshopper on the surface of the water, wondering whether to jump.

Fresh Mongolian Prairie Dog Bait

BILL HEAVEY

I came to Mongolia to fly-fish for *taimen*, the legendary salmonlike fish that lives in its big rivers. When fly-fishing didn't work, I tried spinning with lures. When spinning with lures got no bites, I tried half a dead *lenok* (another kind of fish). When the *lenok* was a bust, I went to the can't-miss bait: a prairie dog. And now, in the last hours of the last day, the dead prairie dog at the end of my line was mocking me.

After five hours of continuous casts into the Delger River without so much as a nibble, the dog was both absurdly stiff and very heavy, the twin effects of rigor mortis and being waterlogged. And though it had been dead for almost 24 hours, it somehow stuck out its stiff, black tongue at me.

"Sure, I'm dead," it seemed to say, "but you are one sorry-ass fisherman. You couldn't catch a *taimen* if you were both in the same bathtub."

"Shut up," I replied. "I may catch one yet." I took another step downriver and cast once more into the water and started another retrieve. I was so far gone by this point that it didn't even strike me as strange that I was conversing with my bait. Because the dog had a point. I had traveled half-way around the world on the trip of a lifetime, fished my brains out for six days, and been skunked.

THE JOURNEY FROM MORON
Looking back, there were signs—like the name of the Mongolian town

from which I embarked on a six-day hunt for big *taimen*: Moron. But I was too pumped to be suspicious. After reading about *taimen* for years, I was finally going after one of the least known gamefish on earth. And after 48 hours on airplanes, I had finally made it to Mongolia, one of the most isolated and unspoiled countries on the planet.

The fish that had prompted me to take leave of my senses is an evil-tempered, prehistoric critter that lives only in certain big, cold, fast rivers in Mongolia and Siberia, most of which flow into the Arctic Ocean. *Hucho hucho taimen* is a spotted fish that grows to a great size (fish measuring more than 4 feet and 50 pounds are not uncommon). Because *taimen* (pronounced TIE-men) live in such remote areas, they are little studied, and sport fishing for them is a recent development. The current all-tackle record, a 92½-pounder caught in Siberia in 1993, is likely nowhere near the maximum size. There is, for instance, a report of a 231-pound commercially caught fish back in 1943. It is an ancient species, the ancestor of modern salmon and trout, equipped with an oversize mouth lined with rows of small, sharp teeth. And it is belligerence personified, cannibalizing its smaller brethren and happily murdering pike, salmon, grayling, small birds . . . and prairie dogs.

I'd read online that Mongolian nomads hook a dog, float it downstream on a shingle of wood, and then give the string a quick jerk. In a typical take, the *taimen* leaps clear of the water *before* attacking its prey, stuns it with a blow from its powerful tail, and then comes back around to finish the job.

The idea of catching a sociopathic aquatic vertebrate like that on a gentlemanly 9-weight fly rod appealed to me. It would be like putting on a top hat and tails and going 10 rounds with the Rock in a phone booth.

I booked a trip with guide Andrew Parkinson through WadersOn .com, a worldwide fishing resource based in the United States. And now I was bouncing over the Mongolian steppe in a van with him and three other anglers: Greg and Bruce (two Aussies on a six-week fishing trip to Mongolia, Alaska, and the Kamchatka Peninsula), and Steven, a Canadian working in Beijing. Even in my jet-lag-diminished state, I was struck by the landscape. But it wasn't so much what was there as what was not.

There were no signs, no fences, no concrete—and, just to keep things simple, no road. Only endless rolling grasslands over which our driver raced. Mongolia, sandwiched strategically between Russia and China, is a huge place, three times the size of France with a population of just 2.75 million, of whom 43 percent are nomadic. Herds of sheep, goats, shaggy yaks, and tough little horses dotted the land.

We passed ancient piles of stones, the altars of invaders who had come and gone as long as 4,000 years ago. Prairie dogs and big marmots streaked for the safety of their dens as they caught sight of the van. Overhead flew ravens and rare white-naped cranes, which number just 5,000 worldwide.

"Just hope Ganchuluun doesn't see a wolf," Parkinson said of our driver. "If a Mongolian in a car or on a horse sees a wolf, he goes a bit mad. And he won't stop until the car is broken, the horse can't run anymore, or the wolf is dead. Mongolians absolutely hate wolves."

We stopped to view deer stones, upright grave markers from the Bronze Age. They all faced south and were covered with stylized images of elk-like deer antlers. On one Parkinson pointed out what he thought was a fishhook. Every few miles we came across gers, the traditional round, felt houses that nomadic herders have been picking up and moving every few months for centuries, forever in search of new grass.

A LOG WITH FINS

We finally got to camp, a series of gers along the banks of the Delger River, late in the afternoon. Over dinner, Parkinson told us about the biggest taimen he'd caught. He and a friend had been prospecting a new river when they spotted a log in the shallow water at the head of an island. Logs being scarce in Mongolia, they inspected this one more closely and determined that it had fins. The friend tried to reach it with his fly rod and failed. Parkinson had a spinning rod and cast a mouse lure in front of the fish.

It made the classic *taimen* attack, leaping clear and clubbing the fish with its tail. Unfortunately, it snapped the 20-pound-test line in the process. Parkinson next tied on a Rapala, and this time the line held. He fought the fish for over an hour as it leapt and raced seven times up and down a side channel of the river. His shoulder and arm went numb during the fight, and his friend massaged them whenever the fish went down to sulk.

At last they fought the fish into shallow water. Because it was too big for their net, they beached it. Parkinson's friend was an experienced angler, but he'd never tangled with a *taimen*, and Parkinson had to talk him into approaching. They measured it at 53 inches. It broke their handheld scales, which maxed out at 50 pounds. That was when Parkinson decided to chuck his job as a farming consultant back in England and move to Mongolia.

LET THE GAMES BEGIN

The next day we started fishing. *Taimen* like big pools and long riffles, Parkinson told us, but since they could be picky, it was necessary to methodically cover every foot of water. We'd be fishing big gurglers, foam-and-bucktail flies that made an appropriately desperate-sounding *plonk* when popped.

All of us piled into the back of an old Zil 31, a six-wheeled army truck that Parkinson said had "fallen out of the back of a Russian army depot" about the time the Soviets pulled out of Mongolia around 1990. We dropped the two Aussies and Edward, a friend of Parkinson's who had come over from England to guide on the trip, downstream. Steven and I got off with Parkinson a couple of miles upstream. During the next eight hours, we experienced a sampling of Mongolian summer: 50-degree swings in temperature accompanied by sun, rain, snow, hail, and winds that rotated through all four points of the compass.

The river was 100 to 150 yards across, but the current in most places was so strong I found it impossible to wade past my knees. Even though the wind made for tough casting, I managed to work a long pool 30 feet out. The drill was to cast across, strip methodically, let the fly sit for a moment as it dangled at the end of its drift, move a step downstream, and repeat. Steven and I did that for three hours without so much as a rise. Then it was time for lunch.

When the truck rumbled up, Greg and Bruce were already in back, smiling. Each had landed and released a *taimen*. The bigger, Greg's, had gone 30 inches. "Just amazing, mate," he told me. "Hit it not 4 feet from me at the end of the retrieve and scared me to death. Vicious fish. Took me 15 minutes to land it, and 30 inches is a small one." He reported the teeth to be sharp and numerous and was glad he'd had Parkinson's biteproof fish-handling glove to remove the fly.

HOLD THE DOG

At lunch in the ger where we took our meals, Parkinson and some of the English-speaking locals he hires gave us a lesson in ger etiquette. Upon entering through the ridiculously low door, you move to your left, clockwise, so as not to impede the universal flow of energy.

You never step on the threshold, touch other people's hats, or use a knife to cut in the direction of any other person. If you spill any beverage, it is customary to immediately shake the hand of the person nearest you. It is considered rude to pass directly in front of an older person, point your feet at the stove, or put water or garbage on a fire, which the Mongolians consider sacred.

When approaching a traditional nomad's ger, the correct greeting is "*Nokhoi khor*," which literally means "hold the dog." A dog in this country is expected to earn its keep, which involves biting the legs off any unknown human. Nyamaa, a beautiful woman who helped around the camp and spoke some English, further informed us that women, especially those who are pregnant, do not eat fish. Fish are the only animal that makes no noise, and the fear is that a woman who eats them may give birth to a deaf child.

WITCHCRAFT?

That afternoon, Greg and Bruce both caught and released small (25-inch) *taimen*. "I don't understand it," Greg said happily over a cold can of Chingis beer. "I'm the worst caster in the lot. I think it's my lucky Filson hat." I smiled. I wanted that hat—I wanted anything that might help me nail a *taimen*.

The morning of the second day I spent fishing some beautiful water, a bend in a small gorge with very fishy-looking pools. Nyamaa was walking some distance behind to keep an eye on me. The Delger, like most rivers in Mongolian, has few particularly dangerous rapids, but on the other hand it's big water, powerful in places, and cold. If you filled your waders, you could get into trouble a lot faster than you could get out.

I had worked a long section and then walked back up to fish it again.

Seated on a rock a little above me, Nyamaa watched in silence. As I passed her, I turned from the river for a moment and teasingly asked, "So what did you do with all the fish?" as if she'd somehow spirited them away. At that instant, as my fly lay motionless at the end of its drift, a *taimen* hit the lure like a baseball bat and disappeared. Frantic, I cast repeatedly, trying to draw another strike. No dice. I looked at Nyamaa, who was smiling enigmatically. Her poise at that moment was unnerving, almost as though she had known the fish would pick that moment to strike.

My intention all along had been to take the high road, fly-fishing only. By the third day, however, I had begun to slide. I accepted Parkinson's offer of a spinning rod and a large, articulated black-and-silver Rapala rigged with two single barbless hooks. This way I could cover more water and fully expected another baseball-bat strike at any moment. Wading out as deep as I dared toward a bend where a glacier came into the river on the far side, I let fly. As a lure wobbled seductively in a foamy pool, another *taimen* came up and exploded. It did everything but actually bite the lure.

Again, my efforts to raise a second strike failed. *Taimen* were aggressive but wary. Parkinson was as disappointed as I was, the sign of a good guide. "My aim is to show every angler a meter-long fish," he said. "Usually, I can. We may have to resort to extreme measures." He gave me a version of his mouse lure, which, when wet, weighed several ounces. I actually threw it over the river and landed it on the glacier, from which I teased it into the water. Still no luck.

At lunch we found out that Greg had hit the jackpot, landing a taimen measuring just over 40 inches and so broad across the back that he couldn't grab it. "I've never seen a freshwater fish like it," he said. While trying to free his lure, he had reached into the fish's mouth with the protective glove. "It nearly crushed me hand," he said. "And bit through the bloody glove like it was paper. Lucky I only got this." He showed a small puncture wound on his finger. I wanted a wound like that, too.

LUCK WITH LENOK

At lunch that day as we sat by the river eating sandwiches, Nyamaa urged me to have a beer. "It will make fish come. I am sure of it." I had the beer. When I woke up, I was lying in the grass and everybody had headed off fishing. Nyamaa was watching me. "You were really asleep. We tried shaking you but you would not awaken. So we take your picture. Did you dream of a fish?" I couldn't remember. She still had that unnerving smile. I got my rod and started casting.

In my obsessive hunt for *taimen*, I'd been passing up all sorts of other opportunities, from fishing for lenok and grayling to visiting a local village and the gers of nearby nomads. One afternoon, we went way upriver and crossed in a spot so deep that the water came up over the floorboards in the back of the truck and it appeared that we might be stationing a casting platform there permanently. As I walked back to the rendezvous point, I discovered Bruce casting in a pool with a little 5-weight. He offered to let me have a try, and within 15 minutes I'd landed two lenok and two grayling, good additions to the night's dinner. It was also the first tug on my line I'd felt since leaving home. I liked it. *Lenok* are quite good sport on a light rod, but I was a prisoner to my *taimen*-mania.

Parkinson, sensing my fixation and my despair, cut the smaller *lenok* in half and rigged the tail end on his spinning rod with a treble hook. I'd slipped from fly-fishing to spinning with lures to heaving a bloody hunk of fish across the river. It wasn't the first time I'd thrown my dignity out of the boat to lighten the load, and it wouldn't be the last.

YOU SHOULDA BEEN HERE NEXT WEEK

On the evening before my last day of fishing, I saw two of the camp boys on horseback trotting swiftly back to camp carrying something hanging from a string. As they got closer, I saw that it was a freshly snared prairie dog. My heart soared. I was so happy I nearly dropped my beer. Prairie dogs are cute little things, and were it not for the fact that they are known to carry bubonic plague and dig horse-crippling holes in the ground, I might have regretted this one's demise.

Parkinson and the boys spent about an hour working on the dog, fortifying its spine and rigging the treble hook until the lure swam with a lifelike motion. They put a good dollop of Gink on the tail to make it float realistically. This, I was sure, was going to be one of those trips that is saved at the last minute with the catching of a tremendous fish. Mine would be a tale told around the campfire for years to come.

Only it didn't turn out that way. I cast that damn prairie dog until we both looked about equally beat up. I never got a bite. As the evening grew gray and the wind came up, Parkinson came and put a hand on my shoulder. "We know there are fish here. And you fished harder than just about anybody I've ever had on a trip." I turned and tried to smile.

The next day, we loaded up and left. The last image I saw of camp was Nyamaa and her benign, knowing smile. We said good-bye at the Moron airport as another group of anglers got off the plane we were about to board.

I got an e-mail from Parkinson the next week. Fishing had turned fantastic right after we left. His four clients landed 18 *taimen* in five days. Each had one that measured at least a meter. I'm trying to be philosophical about it. I find beer helps.

It Sounds So Much Better When You Say *Mal de Mer*

RICHARD GOODMAN

I went to the South of France in the fall of 1991 to research a book on the fishermen who work on the Mediterranean. Years earlier, I'd written a memoir called *French Dirt* about a small village in Provence, and I was trying to recreate that experience—this time on the sea.

I naively fancied myself a sort of prodigal fisherman, somehow capable of understanding the dying breed that plied their trade on the French Mediterranean. At age 15, I'd worked as a bait boy in Virginia for one long hot summer. It was a grueling, messy job, and I was paid in tips only, but I stuck with it.

I moved to Sanary-sur-Mer, a pretty town between Marseille and Toulon, and had moderate success with my initial research. Many of the fishermen were open and helpful, available to indulge me in conversation or take me along on their workday. However, I'd yet to discover the complexity and depth that I believed to be at the heart of this way of life. There was one man among them, a sort of outsider to their fraternity, who seemed more suspicious of my interest. He was one of the few fishermen left who still long-lined for swordfish. In him, I saw what might be the inspiration for my second book.

The best way to begin a description of Nicola Radanovich is with the name of his boat, the *Mistigri*. In colloquial French *Mistigri* means "stray cat." Nicola himself is catlike: sly, alternately alert and dreamy, a big man with a light step. He has a moustache which, when his eyes are crinkled into a smile (as they often are), might be mistaken for whiskers.

He was born in Montenegro, not far from Titograd, in what was once the country of Yugoslavia. At fourteen, he joined the merchant marine and went around the world six times. He'd been to all the celebrated ports: Valparaíso, Leningrad, Shanghai, Glasgow, Havana, Hamburg, Sydney. When he was twenty-one, he came to France to visit an uncle and stayed. During the next ten years he held many jobs, including driving a bus for a second-division rugby team. One day, a player on Nicola's team got sick, and the team manager asked Nicola if he would take the man's place. Though he had never played rugby in his life, he agreed— and wound up playing with the team for seven years.

Eventually he quit the team and settled in Sanary. He went to work as a cook on a pleasure yacht. When he wasn't cooking, he dove for sea urchins. This was illegal; in France, only licensed fishermen may collect them, and one day Nicola was caught. He was taken before the Maritime Board and was about to be fined when an official on the board recognized him. It was a man who had been on Nicola's yacht and enjoyed his cooking.

"I'll tell you what," the official said, "We'll forget about the fine if you become a professional fisherman. We're losing them here in the Var, and we need more." That was all the encouragement Nicola needed. He borrowed money and bought a second-hand fishing boat.

That was nine years ago. Now, I watched from the water's edge as Nicola returned to the quay at Sanary. It was late morning, and he was returning from a night's fishing journey. He tethered his boat to the quay, and unloaded the four long swordfish he had caught. It was a moment of jubilation. People crowded around his boat as he and his crew hauled the dark sleek unicorns from the stern to the quay. The swordfish were so big in some cases, drooping at the center as each man grabbed an end, that it looked as if a dead person were being unloaded. Thirty or forty gawkers took photographs and reached forward to touch the coarse, gray skin and long blade. The men placed the fish on the stand where Nicola's wife immediately sawed thick slices from the corpse, the lovely rose meat went for sale at roughly ten dollars a pound. Nicola, looking bleary after twenty hours at sea, lit a cigarette and grinned, pleased with the adulation. His occasion and presence aroused the port, and I wanted to be a part of it. I'd been pleading with Nicola for some time to take me along when he went fishing for swordfish, but he always had a reason that it wasn't the right moment to take me out.

At last, one winter day, he agreed. "Okay, boy," Nicola told me. "To-morrow, if the weather is good, we go." I was to meet him down at the quay at 4 p.m.

It was a clear, sunny afternoon, a beautiful day in the South of France in the dead of winter. I walked along the quay past the mounds of nets and fishing boats tethered to the edge. Out in the harbor, sailboats were moored close together, their masts reaching into the sky like spears. Nicola stood in the stern of the *Mistigri*. He often took some friends along for company, especially during the overnight hunt for swordfish. I saw Roger, the mate, and next to him a big man with a huge shaved head who looked like a giant out of a fairy tale. Also aboard were two younger friends of Nicola's from Aix-en-Provence.

"Hello, boy!" Nicola said to me. I leapt on board and introduced myself to the others. We cast off and edged out of the port. What a splendid afternoon it was! Some days out on the Mediterranean can be like riding a living sapphire, the water so clear and rich, flicking facets of itself up at you. The descending sun brought out the best in the sea. The boat plowed through the translucent violet blue; the white water hissed along the sides.

About an hour from Sanary, Nicola and his mate Roger baited the lines. The method for catching swordfish is simple. A series of some 150 hooks, dangling from a single line, is baited either with three sardines or one horse mackerel. Then they are let out, each spaced roughly 75 feet apart. The line is weighted at various intervals, so that the effect—if you could see underwater—is to make the line into a series of mountains and valleys, one after another.

Roger shot the hooks through the eyes of the fish, and Nicola lead sections of the line out into the water. It took hours to let out the entire line, which was over 2 miles long. By the time they were done, the sun had set. I knew what lay ahead, so I stayed in a semi-protected area near the cabin regarding Roger and Nicola. All the while, the two men from Aix stood forward in the open air watching the sea and the sunset, their shirts unbuttoned, their faces directed toward the waning globe on the horizon.

Darkness came quickly. The temperature dropped. The sky and the water turned to black. Nicola switched on a light in the stern where they worked. The sea became doubtful, growing to greater heights and depths. As Roger and Nicola and the huge man bantered and joked, I saw only the black water swelling and felt only the boat rising and falling.

I was deathly afraid of getting seasick. We had at least twelve hours ahead of us. I had begged Nicola to take me with him and couldn't bear the thought of begging him to take me home. The idea was humiliating to consider. I had to remain calm, and douse the little fires that my mind had started with suffocating orders like "don't think about it! Put your thoughts on something else!" But the boat kept moving, and I couldn't get my stubborn mind off the fact that I was beginning to feel nauseous.

The harsh light illuminated a chunk of black water approaching the stern, oily and cold looking. My mind worked furiously, battling the oncoming weakness in my legs and my urge to vomit. The swell reached the *Mistigri*, and up we went. It was like riding a swing at a playground. As the boat followed the back of the swell, I rose up, too. The arc was high, and the feeling went directly to the back of my neck. I clung to anything I could. The boat plummeted. The power of ascent was overwhelmed by the descent, and a sad thrill went to my stomach. The boat paused. Another wave approached.

Up we went. The boat ascended and ascended and reached a wrenching stop where it seemed the boat was about to double over onto itself. Then down we went. The boat dipped so far that water towered 4 feet above my head—a dark, flinty mass. The pit of my belly felt the descent.

I had not dressed warmly enough; the raw night air invaded everything. In spite of the cold, I broke out in a clammy, dripping sweat. We ascended again, and the movement got into my head. I pressed my back against the cabin wall as the boat climbed the hill of water.

Nicola looked over at me and asked, "Okay, boy?" I gave him an insincere thumbs-up as he staggered around helping Roger bait more hooks. All the while the massive diesel engines hummed its vibrations right through my body.

Down we went. Again I commanded my brain not to think about feeling ill. This time the loss of gravity was painful. Beyond nausea now, I slipped into a waking nightmare or hallucination in which I starred in an urgent, unstoppable drama: I stood before a traffic judge and pleaded with him. He demanded details, details, all in French. This time the descent made me want to move my bowels. I felt as if I had swallowed a gallon of ether.

Up we went. Pause. Down we went. Pause. I looked over at the two young men from Aix-en-Provence and prayed they were sicker than I was. When I saw the defeat on their faces, I felt relief. One of them staggered over to Nicola and whispered into his ear. Nicola looked mildly surprised, then said, "Well, we'll go back in!" He'd finished laying and marking the lines, and so had to wait until dawn. I was grateful that it wasn't I who had capitulated, but much more grateful that we were heading for dry land. Nicola started the engine. I wondered how to tell him that I wouldn't be coming back out. I wondered what this meant for the book I planned to write. Could I be expected to tell this man's story, if I couldn't even spend a few hours in his shoes? I had another waking nightmare about a day-time talk show: I was promoting my best-selling fishing memoir, when suddenly these same Frenchmen on the boat with me now rose up from the studio audience and called me a fraud, said I didn't have the stomach for fishing.

In an hour, we were back at Sanary. It was around 10 o'clock. After some six hours in almost total blackness, the night lights gave the town the garish feeling of an amusement park. I stepped gratefully onto the quay. The stone surface shifted up and down under my foot. I grabbed hold of the metal stand where Nicola's wife sold fish during the day.

"Okay, boy!" Nicola said. "We're going to the National." He meant the Bar National. It was the only place open at this hour in the winter. Nicola wanted to have a few drinks, eat some food and then head back out. The baited lines wouldn't be retrieved until dawn, but he needed to be out there most of the night in case a swordfish struck early. I hadn't told him yet that I wouldn't be getting back on that boat. As I followed Roger and the others, the quay moved askew. I put my foot down, but the hard stone seemed always a foot too low or too high. Nicola grinned and moved with his usual light step.

At the bar, everyone ordered *pastis*. I did, too. This strong, anise-tasting drink was actually a balm. I swallowed it gratefully. The milky fire flowed down my gullet and rescued my gut. I needed it, because the National was moving a bit, too, and I had to lean my elbow on the bar for support. The young men from Aix had already told Nicola they weren't going back out. Now it was my turn.

"Nicola," I said, "I . . . I can't go back out. I'm too sick."

He turned and smiled. "You're joking?"

"No."

Then he wasn't smiling. He looked disappointed and a bit angry, and I felt even more miserable than I already was. I had never seen Nicola look this way, and it was terrible to be the object of his rare displeasure.

"Really?" he said.

"Really." I remembered all the times I'd begged him to take me out, and now I felt ashamed.

"Okay," he said with neutrality that sent a chill through me. He turned to the others. "Let's go."

At the boat, I said goodbye. Roger, the mate, turned to me and said, "When you get into your bed later tonight, think of us."

With the two men from Aix, I watched the boat move slowly through the dark harbor once again, past the still sailboats back out into the open sea. It disappeared into the night.

On the way home, the cobbled street moved under my feet. Back at my apartment, I removed layer after layer of clothing, then took a hot shower. I climbed into bed, still trembling from the night sea air. The cold had seeped through to my marrow. As I pulled the covers up, I heard Roger's voice again, "Think of us when you get into your bed." I fell asleep with relief and shame.

The next day, I walked down to the port at around 10 a.m. to meet the *Mistigri*. I was reluctant, but thought it right to face the men. It was another bright winter day. Nicola's wife waited on the quay. She was a beautiful woman with an easy smile. When she saw me, she looked surprised.

"I thought you were with them," she said, looking outward.

"I was. But I got seasick. When they came in for dinner, I got off."

She looked at me with contempt. I shrugged stupidly.

Soon, the boat arrived. The men got off, and I saw they had caught just one small swordfish. Nicola saw me, but barely acknowledged my presence. Looking tired, he and the mate unloaded the fish and brought it to the stand. Nicola's wife immediately sawed and sold portions to the assembled crowd. Soon, the jostling people obscured my view of Nicola and Roger. I turned and walked away, mulling over ideas for other possible books. French shepherds or cheese-makers, perhaps.

I was no fisherman, if I'd ever had any doubts.

The Cuban Classic

BILL HEAVEY

I came to Cuba after hearing a number of things too interesting to ignore. One is that there are serious bass anglers and some big fish down here. The other is that the national tournament is almost exactly like the Bassmaster Classic except for a few details. Instead of having $50,000 rocket sleds, the anglers fish from rowboats. All fishing is catch-and-kill. (Protein is relatively hard to come by in Cuba, and the idea of returning it to the water has not even gotten off the ground yet. The fish go to either the anglers themselves or the Cuban Federation of Sport Fishing folks who work the competition.) And instead of the winner's getting half a million bucks—and many times that in endorsements and appearance fees—the top angler and team take home nothing more than a rinky-dink plastic trophy and bragging rights to being the best bass fisherman in the country.

I am more than a bit nervous on the 500-mile drive across a good chunk of the country from Havana to Bayamo. The guys I'm going to meet are fellow bass anglers, of course. But they are also Cuban. I, on the other hand, am a citizen of *El Empirio*—as they refer to their northern neighbor—the most powerful country on earth.

As we enter the city and my anxiety about meeting the thirty-two anglers competing in the Cuban national bass tournament rises, I tell my guide and translator, Samuel Yera, to stop at a gas station so I can arm myself with the one thing that bridges all socioeconomic barriers—beer. Samuel is a three-time tournament winner who failed to qualify this year because he spent too much time guiding saltwater clients for tarpon (which is why he is available to guide and translate for me). Ready with packs of cold Bucanero Fuerte, we park at the government dormitory by the local baseball stadium and head upstairs, guided by the sound of men's voices spilling out of an open door.

MEET THE CHAMPIONS

"Sam-well!" calls a man sitting on his bunk when he catches sight of my host. A burly shirtless guy with a farmer's tan, still dripping from a shower, he waddles over to embrace Yera. The men are sitting in the room, passing around a bottle of rum. Everyone crowds about their old friend, who is regarded as perhaps the most knowledgeable bass fisherman in Cuba.

He introduces me all around, and I shake hard, calloused hands. They are carpenters, security guards, and paper-mill workers. One is a local plastic surgeon, another a railroad engineer, another an artist. Special passes from the government allow them to be absent from work for the tournament. American anglers ready themselves for competition by studying the lake and fine-tuning their GPS settings. These guys have been strengthening their legs, backs, and especially their hands. The last thing the men want is blisters or fatigue slowing them down as they row to and from a spot that might hold a kicker fish on the three-bass stringer that each will weigh in.

I pass out beer and survey the room: eight beds with about 2 feet of hanger space in between, a bathroom off the end, a tiny porch outside. Some men have two rods, some just one, plus a little tackle box of some sort and, neatly ironed, the shirt and pants they will wear on the water. Some have an everyday ball cap and a special one with a fish on it for tournament finery. It strikes me that these guys, the top bass anglers in Cuba, have less gear than an average 10-year-old in the States.

Samuel is soon lost to me, deep in rapid conversation with a knot of anglers. They don't speak English and I don't *habla español*, but through smiles and gestures we find ways to communicate. One of the younger guys, with curly black hair and a Red Sox cap, motions me over to show off the plastic worms that he, like many others, makes himself. He uses dental clay to shape a mold of the bait to be copied, then melts down old lures, scrap plastic, whatever he can find. He mixes that with some kind of oil, heats it, and pours it into the mold. The result is a worm that looks surprisingly true to the original, right down to the faint Power Bait lettering on the tail.

The 9-inch black worm he displays has a few flecks of rubber where it shouldn't, but it will certainly catch fish. My new friend with the handmade worms is curious about something. Through Samuel, he asks my opinions: Do I prefer the Mann's Augertail worm to that company's Jelly worm? The Augertail has more flutter, of course, but sometimes the subtler action of the Jelly worm is better in heavy cover. I interrupt the translation to throw my hands up in despair. "Who the hell knows!" I find myself nearly shouting. I feel as if I've stumbled into some inverted reality—Alice in Bassland. "Besides, you know more about American baits than I do!" I take an equilibrium-restoring swig of the rum.

THERE HAS BEEN A SMALL CHANGE

Samuel informs me that there has been a change for tomorrow. The government promised sixteen rowboats for the tournament but has delivered only eight. So the two-day event will now run over four days, the field alternating until everybody gets two full days on the water. In the United States, this would have provoked charges that the tournament was no longer fair. Not least among the reasons: An approaching cold front promises a difficult bite for whoever is on the water when it arrives.

But we are not in the United States, and so four days it will be. Actually, rowboats are quite a luxury, according to Samuel. "Most of our tournaments are done either wading or fishing from inner tubes."

Some of the men, he tells me, are market fishermen. They rise before dawn to bicycle to local lakes, spending all day kicking around the water. Eight or ten hours later, they deflate their tubes and ride home carrying rod, tackle, fins, tube, and their catch. This sounds like it would be fun for a while. To do it every day, to *have* to do it, might not be.

I look around the room and notice the oars in the corners. For this, the national championship, each team has to bring their own. One set with aluminum shafts leans against the wall, but the others are completely homemade, poles with splits of roughly shaped wood nailed or screwed to the shafts. Two pairs sport blades of corrugated aluminum, a common roofing material, that has been hammered more or less flat.

The mood in the room is relaxed and happy. Tomorrow, on the water, they will compete. But for now they are celebrating having made the cut and seeing old friends. Samuel says there are about 80,000 members of the Cuban Federation of Sport Fishing, the organization that sponsors tournaments, of which number he believes 30,000 are bass anglers.

"But this is the most important tournament in Cuba, because we believe bass are the hardest fish, the most sporting. It's a big honor to the winner." The tournament began in 1969, and this is the twenty-fifth time it has been held on Lake Leonero in rural Granma province. When the rum reaches me again, I take another swig, grimace, and pretend to suffer mild convulsions. "Ah," I finally gasp. "*Qué bueno!*" They laugh. Maybe I'm okay after all.

Some of the rods, I notice, are rigged with neon-bright orange or yellow line. I ask Samuel if the bright line doesn't spook fish. "You don't understand," he says, smiling. "Here there is no learning curve. The first time a fish gets caught is also the last time." One guy suddenly discovers something beneath his bed and holds it up with a cry of exclamation. It's a coconut shell filled with flowers, bird feathers, colored stones, and a tangle of old fishing line. "*Santeria!*" he announces—the Cuban folk religion that blends Christianity and African animistic beliefs, including the power of charms and spirits. Someone has put it there to jinx him. He deadpans that his skill is such that he will defy witchcraft. The room erupts in loud, friendly derision.

NOT YOUR AVERAGE YANQUI BASS TOURNAMENT

Samuel and I seem to be doing an odd little dance. The deal is that I hold up lures for his inspection and he keeps shaking his head. He negates a 4-3D 8-inch jointed Rapala. He turns down a 6-inch bubble-gum floating worm. "Bigger," he says. We're in a motorized skiff on Lake Leonero. The anglers, two-man teams from Cuba's fourteen provinces (plus an extra team from the host province and one from the Island of Youth, off Cuba's southern coast), are spread out over the lake somewhere around us.

I'm here to watch the fishermen, but Samuel says we need to keep our distance from them, especially on the first day. "The fish and the anglers are both very sensitive to noise." This, I am pretty sure, is bull. I think Samuel just wants to catch some fish, partly to ease his obvious chagrin at not being in the race, and partly because he is just a diehard bass man.

And the bass on Leonero like their baits not only big but apparently disruptive too, because the lure that finally gets the nod is a no-name Devil's Horse-style topwater. This fat cigar of a bait has propellers fore and aft, and treble hooks the size of little chandeliers. It's so big and raucous that I've never even been tempted to tie it on. But Samuel likes it.

"Now you're speaking," he says. I ask why the fish here prefer big lures and whether that is the case all over Cuba. "It's not," he replies. "Some places you need small lures. And I don't even know the reason they prefer the big lures on this lake. They just do."

The morning is calm; a light wind ripples the water. Using Samuel's baitcasting reel and a 6-foot rod, I cast and retrieve. The lure is wiggling like some hyperactive dachshund that fell off the dock when a bass engulfs it. It disappears in a sudden sinkhole of water and I set the hook, the fish diving, pulling left, heading for the pads. I turn it and bring it in. It's the gamest 2-pounder I've ever tangled with—fat, healthy, and thoroughly ticked off at having a hook in its mouth. Samuel is casting a large Zara Spook on a big spinning rod, and soon both of us are catching fish every second or third cast, a number of which run 3 pounds.

It's crazy-good video-game fishing, the flat-out most sustained largemouth action I've ever had. After about ten minutes of this, Samuel stows his rod. "No good here," he says. I ignore him, cast again, and ask if he'd mind explaining just what the Sam Hill he's talking about. "Place like this, you can wear your arm out. But you can't win a tournament."

What, I ask, would it take to win?

"Here? You need an average of 5 pounds each fish to be competitive. To win, it usually takes an average of 6 pounds, maybe a little more." I look at him. He's smiling but he's not kidding.

We need to invade this country.

HAVING FUN

We move the boat. It is January, and the females are getting ready to spawn, Samuel says. He is looking for a certain water color that he says the bass prefer. "Where it is coffee-colored—you see over there?—you will not find fish. And often the big females nest in the open water, away from the pads. Often they like green hydrilla flats if you are just fishing the structure you see, you will not get them."

We keep moving.

At last he anchors near a big flat off a channel. On my fourth cast, something smashes my lure. "Big bass!" Samuel says. "Big bass!" It bends my short baitcasting rod nearly double before I get it to the boat. It has a mouth like a trash can. Samuel says it's a 7-pounder. That would make it the second-biggest bass of my life. I catch two 5-pounders over the next fifteen minutes.

"Having fun?" asks Samuel.

On the way back to the put-in, we cruise by some of the competitors. Most are scattered over a single area, a large bowl surrounded by endless pads. One boat, however, is off by itself, fishing a more distant edge of lily pads. It's the team from Las Tunas, a neighboring province, an experienced duo that is expected to do well here. The guy at the oars stops when he sees us, calls to Samuel, stands, and struggles to hoist a stringer that's so heavy it's all he can do to lift it clear of the water. There are about ten fish on it, big oblong bass. One will go nearly 10 pounds, another just over 7.

In the United States, you no longer see such a sight. That's a good thing, of course. Any lake would get fished out fast if it were subject to a sustained harvest of its biggest bass. On the other hand, it's something to behold. The guys will winnow the catch down to six, three per angler. The biggest looks to be a 10-pounder. There are two others that will go close to 7.

The Las Tunas guys tell Samuel that they lost two big fish, one of which would have gone 10, when the line got tangled up with the anchor rope. They have caught virtually all their fish on big worms. And they are fishing them in a way I've never seen.

The guy in the bow has a 9- or 10-inch dark worm Texas-rigged on what looks to be a 3/0 offset worm hook with about a 1D 8-ounce sinker.

He has a 7-foot spinning rod, which he uses to throw the worm as far as he can. Then he reels it steadily back, just like a crankbait. On his fourth cast, he suddenly stops reeling at what must be a strike of some kind. He pauses for just a second, lowers the rod, reels in slack, then sets the hook hard. His line begins to dance, and soon he is boating another 5- or 6-pound fish.

I have Samuel ask him what the take is like. "Just the sensation of weight, or maybe a tap," he translates. "Nothing strong. They inhale it, not bite it. You give them a moment, take the slack, and hook them." The guy says they fish the worm higher or lower in the water column as conditions dictate. "We fish always this worm," one of them, Onix Hernandez, says. "If I see a fish hitting the poppers of other fishermen, I just fish it closer to the surface." They never let it hit bottom and never stop reeling unless they feel a fish. I've never heard of crankbait-style worming. But many things, I'm learning, are different in Cuba. And it's awfully hard to argue with what works.

Back on shore, the boats are pulling in to the mud bank that is the landing area. Pigs and chickens run around, looking for any crumbs dropped from lunch bags. The Las Tunas team shows me its worms: all hand-poured and rigged on homemade light football-type jigheads. Their fish are still on the stringer in the water. Most of the fishermen are playing it close to the vest, keeping their stringers submerged. This is partly to keep the fish wet as long as possible—they won't be officially weighed here but back in Bayamo, a two-hour drive during which the fish will be out of water. And it's partly just to keep other teams guessing about how they did.

That afternoon, in a small square in the dusty city, the official weigh-in finally takes place on old-fashioned mechanical scales might have been borrowed from a fruit stand. Moving away from the pack has paid off for Las Tunas. They are in first place with six fish weighing 38 pounds, more than 6 pounds ahead of the second-place team, Villa Clara, which has 31 pounds. One of the Granma anglers has his photo taken with a fish of just over 10 pounds, the biggest bass caught in a tournament on Leonero in years. The guys who didn't get to fish today look grave. 38 pounds is not unheard of, but it will be tough to equal, let alone surpass.

THE BEAUTY OF THE UGLY STIK

On the second day—my last, since I had only expected to be here for a two-day tournament—Samuel once again takes me fishing because of his commendable wish not to disturb the other anglers. Once again, I'm using his baitcaster, while he uses the big spinning rod. I tried the latter for a couple of casts and disliked it. It's too big, too heavy, not particularly sensitive, and a lot of work to crank. He hefts the rod. "It's what every Cuban asks his family or friends in the States to bring him," he says. "Seven-foot medium-heavy Ugly Stik spinning rod with a Penn 7500 SS."

"Why?"

He hefts it again, working a topwater. "Durability," he says. "An Ugly Stik is like a '57 Chevrolet. Almost indestructible." I look at the Penn reel, all 25.5 ounces of it, with its measly three ball bearings. "A Cuban would take this over a Shimano or a Daiwa every time," he adds. "Very dependable. Goes forever. And easy to work on." He grunts, sets the hook, and pulls in a 5-pounder. "Time to move. Look for the big ones."

We don't find the big ones, but we do tire our arms our on the 2- to 4-pounders. And there are worse ways to spend a day. As we head back toward shore, we pass not too far from one of the two teams from Granma province. One evidently has a big fish on because he is excitedly telling his co-angler to get the net. But the net man lunges at the fish awkwardly, frightening it. The fish jumps close to the boat, and the line goes slack. Both men slump back to their seats, despairing at having lost what was obviously a huge bass. Samuel shakes his head in commiseration. "It's just because they're not used to boats, not used to nets. We don't carry nets when we wade or tube. That fish, it could have won them the tournament maybe."

It could have, but it didn't. A few days after I arrive back in the United States, I get an e-mail from Samuel. Las Tunas won the tournament with a two-day, twelve-fish total of 78 pounds 8 ounces. Granma was just 5 ounces behind. The fifth-place team, he writes, from his home province of Villa Clara, should have finished in third place. "They had an 11- or 12-pound fish on a big Husky Jerk. But it made one last run by the boat and opened the treble hook and escaped."

On my last evening in Bayamo, I am once again sitting on the end of a bed drinking beer with the guys while a bottle of rum slowly laps the room. I have brought an entire duffel bag of plastics, lures, and line cadged from Yamamoto, Berkley, and Rapala. I dump it out on the floor and it vanishes in the time it takes a school of piranhas to clean a cow carcass. The only problem is that most of the plastics are tiny, 6 inches or less. No matter. Some anglers are even now squeezing the packs to gauge how well they will melt down to be recast into larger baits.

One of the guys from Granma can't even wait that long. He pulls a 4-inch Senko (green pumpkin) from its pack, steadies it, hefts it experimentally. Then he cuts the first 3 inches off one of his 9-inch black worms with a knife, carefully heats both the cut tip of the worm and one end of the Senko with his lighter, and presses the two together until they cool. The result is a 10-inch, two-tone hybrid ribbon tail. He smiles, wiggles it seductively, lifts it for my inspection.

"Beel," he asks. "What you think?" I give him a thumbs-up and a smile, already vowing never to throw away a chewed-up worm again.

"Oh yeah. They'll clobber that thing."

Fish Fry

MICKEY WRIGHT

Grandpa called all the uncles, aunts, nieces, nephews, cousins, and other friends and kin and told them, "I'm hosting the picnic this year at the lake. And it won't be hot dogs and hamburgers. We're going to have us a heap of deep-fried perch fillets. I'll catch a pile of them."

There were two areas in which Grandpa's hubris always got the better of him: fishing and practical jokes. His younger brother Johnny was his arch nemesis in both respects. If Grandpa didn't deliver on the fish, Johnny would be there to ride him mercilessly.

Characteristically overconfident, Grandpa waited until the day before the picnic to go after the fish. Pressed for time and hungry for perch, Dad and I went along. The collection of stuffed fish hanging in grandpa's den was less a history of what he had caught than what he had wanted to catch.

The morning started well enough. A light fog drifted over the calm water, and dew covered the aluminum boat. I checked my seat cushion before I sat—a habit learned over years of fishing with Grandpa. He often booby-trapped the seats with whoopee cushions or rubber snakes. Grandpa gave me a sly wink when he caught me looking. I felt safe then; if he'd planned something, he would have kept a poker face.

Grandpa fired up the outboard. Dad sat in the bow and I in the middle seat. It may have been Dad's boat, but it was Grandpa's show. He ran the motor, picked the spots, and fished from the choice seat at the stern. It had always been that way.

Dad caught two perch within the first five minutes. After that, things didn't just slow down, they came to a screeching halt. We fished for another two hours without even a nibble. We switched spots, tried different baits and lures, even said a prayer or two. Grandpa muttered more than he prayed and cussed once or twice, as well. He fished facing away from me, but his head sank between his shoulders and his ears turned bright red: a sure sign of his frustration.

Normally, while fishing with Grandpa, he'd tell stories, such as the time at duck camp when he set the alarm clock three hours ahead and Uncle Johnny ended up sitting in a duck blind at 3 a.m. wondering why the sun wasn't coming up. But with only two fish on the stringer, this outing had turned somber.

Another fishless hour passed, and the prospect of hotdogs and hamburgers replacing perch on the menu loomed ominously. At last, Grandpa revealed that he had one more secret spot.

"It's a real honey hole," he told us. "I've never shown it to a soul, and neither one of you better tell anyone about it, especially not Johnny." He chuckled and said, "Johnny told me he was going to fish here once when we were kids. I beat him out there and dropped cherry bombs in the water for ten minutes. He didn't catch a thing." Grandpa laughed aloud at the memory of his prank. It was the happiest he'd been all morning. "That was a long time ago," he said, in a quieter voice.

Grandpa motored us to where a rock ledge plunged into deep water. He circled the boat around three times. Satisfied with our location, he dropped the anchor.

We fished there for a half hour with no luck. Grandpa started grumbling again. His ears turned red.

Dad tapped my shoulder and winked, putting his finger to his lips. Quietly he pulled up the stringer and took off one of the perch he had caught, hooked it to his line and dropped it overboard.

Grandpa, facing out the back of the boat, didn't see.

"Eh heh!" Dad grunted. "Got one."

He reeled it in, unhooked it and handed it to me. I re-hooked it to my line and dropped it in.

"Got one." I shouted.

Back and forth we went taking turns re-catching those same two perch. We even hooked on both of them at the same time for "doubles."

"I told you boys this was a honey hole." Grandpa boasted. He was so proud of his fish-finding prowess, it never dawned on him that he had not caught a single fish while Dad and I were "catching" them left and right.

"We're going to have us a fish fry!" said Grandpa gleefully.

After another ten "catches" those poor perch lips were pretty perforated, so Dad decided to let them rest in peace. We put them back on the stringer.

After fifteen minutes passed with no action, Grandpa decided we had enough fish to fry and motored us back to the dock.

"Well boys," he said, tying up the boat. "We better get to cleaning this mess of fish."

Dad and I broke up laughing and showed him the two ragged perch on the stringer.

All the color drained from Grandpa's face as he looked at those two fish. I suddenly felt sorry for what we had done. Not only had his fishing crown been swiped from under him, but he'd been out-pranked as well.

"Oh well," he composed himself after a few moments of silence. "I suppose if I'm going to be had, I'd rather it be by you two than by Johnny."

Our extended family was a little disappointed by picnic offerings of hot dogs and hamburgers, but with the added spice of our fish story the fare tasted just fine. As for those two perch, I gutted and cleaned them and Johnny cooked them up. When he served them to Grandpa, the whole family gathered round and ribbed him so persistently that he lost his appetite.

Appearances

ROBERT H. JONES

Below me, a faded red canoe drifted slowly off the bay's rocky shoreline, its lone occupant wielding his fly rod with practiced skill and grace. Ralph lives and works shifts in the city, but spends weekends and holidays at his cabin on the shore of the bay. No one knows the lake as well as Ralph, so I readied my camera. The afternoon light was good, and it probably wouldn't take long before I got some action shots of him fighting a fish. Through my lens, I could see the overgrown whiskers on his face. Ralph is a confirmed bachelor who dresses like a tramp at his cabin and never shaves.

I perched on a suitable rock while waiting, observing how methodically he prospected each potential location. A few minutes had passed when I detected a faint droning sound. An airplane? No, it was an outboard motor, obviously high-powered, unusual on this small lake. It grew louder, then a wide-bodied boat appeared from around the point. Behind, a water skier was doing an admirable job of maintaining his balance while crisscrossing back and forth, jumping over the wake.

When the boat curved gracefully toward Ralph's canoe on what appeared to be a collision course, I worried that the driver might not see him. Finally the boat veered sharply away. As it roared past, much too close for comfort, the driver and two occupants shouted, simultaneously raising cans of beer in salute. The skier, leaning almost parallel to the water, swung wide, skittering within 20 feet of the canoe as the lacy curtain of water from his skis arced high into the air, totally drenching Ralph. Moments later the boat's wake arrived, almost capsizing him.

As boat and skier faded into the distance, Ralph reeled in his line, laid his rod in the canoe, then picked up his paddle and headed toward the cabin. While watching, I recalled an old joke: if you're fishing and a water skier starts harassing you, give him a cold can of beer—but don't forget to lead him by about 15 feet.

I walked back to my van and drove down the road to the turn-off to Ralph's cabin. By the time I arrived he had changed into dry clothes and was buttoning his shirt.

"Hope you dried behind your ears," I said by way of greeting.

"Yep. I saw you up on the bluff. Spying on me, eh?"

"Nope, taking photographs."

"That right?" Ralph did up the last button. "And what did you photograph?"

"A motor-drive sequence. Ten shots of them buzzing your canoe, and the water skier giving you a bath—which they probably thought you really needed."

"Very funny." Ralph scratched the greying stubble on his chin, then picked up his electric shaver. "Which lens were you using?"

"200."

"Hmm . . . strong enough to read the registration number?"

I nodded. "Even the brand of beer they were drinking."

For the first time since my arrival, Ralph smiled. "Any chance of seeing them when you get the film developed?"

"No problem."

The shaver squealed and rattled like a vacuum cleaner sucking up broken glass, defeating further attempts at conversation. When he finished, Ralph explained that he was off to the city to start a string of evening shifts, but first he planned on stopping by the resort—which has the lake's only boat-launching ramp.

After locking the cabin, we said our goodbyes and strolled to our vehicles. Ralph waved casually and drove off. I sat there for a while, musing over the difference a shave and his sharply pressed Royal Canadian Mounted Police sergeant's uniform makes to my friend's appearance.

Demolition Northern Pike

MICHAEL FEDO

Throughout his adult life, my mother's brother, Howard, was an inveterate angler. He spent many hours on lakes around Duluth, Minnesota, where he took untold numbers of large northern pike and walleyes. Since his wife refused to prepare fish dinners more than once a week, Howard was always dropping off fish for my grandmother and great aunt Hilma, who lived next door to us on Tenth Avenue East. As often as not, he'd leave a few fillets for us, and also for Olga Engqvist, a widow whose house bordered Grandma's to the north.

One afternoon, after Olga thanked him for his gift of fresh pike, she surprised him with a request. "Howard, as much as I appreciate these fish, I'd really like to go with you sometime. I used to get up on Rice Lake with Earl now and again, but I haven't fished even once since he died."

This request did not please my uncle. He told her that the water sometimes got rough, and, if anything should happen, he didn't know if he could keep her afloat.

"I've thought of that," she said. "What I'd really enjoy would be a day of ice fishing next winter." She smiled. "It used to be so cozy in Earl's old fish house. We'd play whist and eat chili and crackers. We'd heat coffee on the stove and bring donuts up from Johanson's Bakery. My, but we had lovely times."

Howard attitude softened when he heard the menu and he tentatively agreed to find a day to take Olga along sometime in the future.

He no doubt expected Olga would forget about ice fishing, but right after Christmas she called and reminded him of his promise. He told her they should wait out the cold snap, because with temperatures around 20 below zero, it would be hard to keep the fish house warm, and there'd be real trouble if the car wouldn't start because of the frigid weather. "Folks have been known to freeze like a side of beef in weather like this," he said, hoping she'd abandon her ice fishing notion.

But Olga didn't waver. Just as soon as the thermometer inched above zero, she called him again.

"Might as well make it Saturday," he said, reluctantly. "Weather man says it could warm up to 5 or 10 above."

Olga didn't want to be the only woman on the ice, so she told Howard she would see if my great aunt Hilma might agree to come along. She hurried next door, quite excited about the prospects of catching some whoppers.

It was the 1950s and I was about twelve. I'd just dropped off Grandma's grocery order from Paulson's Super Value on Ninth Street.

Olga, sitting at the kitchen table, sucked coffee through a sugar cube and told Hilma about the joys of fishing through a hole in the ice in the dead of a Duluth winter.

Hilma, though born in the U. S., retained the pronounced Swedish accent she'd acquired from her Stockholm-born parents. And she thought the whole matter ridiculous. "Ven I vas a girl up to Deerwood, ve used to fish because ve needed food. But to just go out and freeze yourself half to death—vy Olga, you're a bigger fool than I thought."

But Olga persisted as she dunked cookies and crumbed her coffee. "Hilma, we've been neighbors for forty years, and in all that time, you've never had an adventure. We'll have a grand time. We'll bring a nice pot of stew, and there's always fresh coffee. And should you catch a fish, why you'd just drop your teeth. It's such a thrill."

"Vat gave you the idea I vant to catch a fish anyvay, Olga?"

"I have a little philosophy, Hilma. I believe a person has to have new experiences in order to really be alive. You're becoming nothing but an old fuddy-duddy." Olga coughed. "Well, I don't mean that, but I really would enjoy your company, and we'd only be gone a few hours."

Hilma wouldn't commit herself, and over the next several days, Olga kept at her. Finally—surprisingly—Hilma relented.

At the same time, Howard asked me to go along with him in case the ladies needed extra attention. "I can't imagine anything worse than being alone out on the ice with those two biddies," he carped.

Olga awaited the day with great anticipation. She came over to Grandma's on Thursday in her ice-fishing attire. The clothing, which had belonged to her late husband, was three sizes too big. She wore a plaid wool shirt and a pair of navy dungarees with the thirteen-button front flap—a relic from Earl's World War One service. The clothes reeked of mothballs. She also wore a red-and-black-checked deerstalker cap, and she carried Earl's old navy pea coat, which dwarfed her, but would keep her warm as toast, she insisted. She had also brought extra clothes that Hilma might like to wear.

"None of that stuff vould fit me," Hilma said. "I guess maybe I von't go. Nothing to vear."

"I bet some of Mom's clothes would fit you," I offered, squelching her excuse.

"Don't bodder your mudder for her tings."

"No bother. I'll get you a nifty outfit for the day."

Finally dressed in borrowed clothes, Hilma did look a bit odd, but no more so than any other sixty-something woman off to do battle with the wintry elements. She wore wool slacks over long underwear, two heavy sweaters, an old baseball jacket of mine, and two thick scarves wrapped around her head.

We departed at 7 a.m. on Saturday for Fish Lake, 15 miles from town, where Howard had arranged for a four-person house. During the drive in Howard's rusty 1939 Plymouth he seemed sullen and the ladies were unusually quiet until a terrible thought crossed Hilma's mind. "I knew there vas something vy I shouldn't go," she cried. "Vere does a person go to the bathroom?"

Howard chuckled. "Why, you have to fend for yourself. Auntie. Adam and Eve didn't have plumbing either. They just went in the woods."

"Sure, if you got voods, that's fine. But you don't got no voods, no toilet paper, nothing. Just ice."

Olga giggled. "Let's cross that bridge if we get to it, Hilma. If worst comes to worst, you can always ask the men to look the other way."

Finally we arrived at the lake, and Howard drove out onto the ice to a fish house about a half-mile from shore. The house was a relatively spacious affair, with a small homemade barrel stove against one wall and a card table in the middle. Four 5-gallon paint containers turned upside down provided seating.

Howard carried in a box of scrap lumber and started the fire; I grabbed the ice chisel and began chopping holes in each corner of the house, and Olga started coffee from lake water.

Soon the fire crackled, and the ladies were seated. Howard and I rigged up the lines, impaling sucker minnows on number 2 hooks and dropping them into the holes. Back then, most ice anglers didn't have reels that worked well in winter. We'd grown accustomed to hand-lining when we went ice fishing. Howard had brought some old fly rod reels and short rods to hold the extra line, but they were of little use when you actually got a strike. The hook was set and the fish was played all by hand.

Howard instructed the women. "When you see your bobber disappear, count to ten and give a hard yank on the line to set the hook." He pantomimed the technique. "Be sure you count to ten or the fish will spit out the hook and you'll lose him." He took his position in one corner and drew a hit from his flask containing schnapps. "It'll warm you quicker than coffee," he said, extending the flask to the ladies, who refused. "Don't suppose either of you chew snoose either then," he teased.

"Ve ain't chewing no tobacco," huffed Hilma, indignant.

"Pardon me, Howard," said Olga, "but how fast should we count to ten?"

Howard groaned. "Oh, take about a second for each count."

"Then I guess I should yank the line right now," she said.

"Not now, Olga. Good heavens, we just got here. I hope you ladies aren't—"

"Well, Howard, that bobber disappeared just as soon as you dropped it in the hold," Olga said. And indeed, line peeled off the crude reel she held in her mittened hand.

"Jerk the line!" I hollered. "Looks like a monster."

Olga reared back and set the hook, and in the process fell off her seat.

Howard moved to aid her. She held tightly to the line, but it still slipped between her fingers. "Careful now, Olga, play him real easy," he said. "We don't want to lose a big fella like this."

"My, is this ever exciting," said Olga. "Is this ever fun." She drew herself up on one knee.

Suddenly the line slackened. "Oh-oh, he's off," Howard said. But, detecting movement in the line, he shouted, "Take in the line, Olga. Quick!"

He began helping Olga tighten the line. The two of them grabbed loose line, dropping it behind them as the fish dashed back toward the hole. About 30 feet of loose line lay in swirls on the floor of the icehouse. "He's running again," Howard hollered, "Give him more line."

"What do you mean, Howard?" Olga shouted.

"Don't hold on so tight. He'll break the line. Here, let me show you." Howard took the line that Olga held and kept tension on it, but let the great fish run. "See, I let him swim, like this. We'll tire him out and then we can bring him in."

"Okay," Olga said. "Let me have the line back. It's my fish, Howard."

"You sure you can handle this? You got maybe a 20- to 25-pound northern on there. I want to make sure you get him here. You'll get your picture in the paper if you catch it, Olga."

"I ain't having my picture took," said Hilma. "Not in these stupid clothes. Olga looks plenty crazy herself in Earl's old get-up."

The fish continued forceful runs out for 15 or 20 feet, then circled toward the hole again. Line passed from Howard to Olga and back again, depending where the great fish surged. Howard was perspiring, and Olga became grim-faced as she kneeled and peered into the dark hole. "If Earl could see this, Howard. This is really something."

"I just hope we can hold him, Olga," Howard said, shaking loose line from his fingers.

"Vun ... two ... tree ... " Hilma counted, staring into her hole. Her line too peeled off the reel. I grabbed it and set the hook into something solid. Then I handed her the line. "Take him in, Hilma."

"Ooooh, he's heavy," Hilma said. Jaws clamped, she made small grunts with each heave on the line.

Howard muttered under his breath, then said, "Geez, what's going on here, Olga? He feels heavier now than before."

He resumed muttering as my bobber disappeared beneath the ice. I grabbed the line, made the set and felt the run of a strong fish.

A moment later, Hilma tried to switch her reel from one hand to the other but the fighting fish jerked it from her grip and it fell into the hole.

"Nuts," she said. "I lost the whole vorks."

"Sorry, Hilma," Howard yelled. "We got all we can handle here."

Hilma shrugged, stepped toward Howard's hole and stopped. "Everyting's going hayvire," she said. "Now your bobber is gone too, Howard."

"Damn it!" Howard cried. "Hold on here, Olga." He dashed for his own hole. "What in God's name is happening, anyway?" he said to no one in particular, and began working his line.

I continued wrestling with my line and saw Hilma's bobber pass beneath my hole. As I drew in my line, her bobber followed. I grabbed it and worked both lines. Then I had an epiphany; this might be just one fish entangled in all our lines.

A give-and-take battle seesawed another five minutes, with the line lying in knotted, twisted coils at our feet. Howard was losing heart. The mess would never unravel even if the fish were landed. He prided himself on maintaining his gear in top condition. Hilma had lost one reel already, and there was no telling the extent of any other damage and possible loss.

Hilma, stepping toward the stove for the coffee pot, became ensnared in the line on the floor and tripped. She stumbled against the wall and knocked the chimney connection from the stove. The house quickly filled with smoke. I kicked open the door to let the smoke escape, but engulfed by acrid fumes, all of us coughed. "Endure, friends, endure," cried Olga. "Hold a damp hankie to your faces." She wasn't about to let that fish go.

"There's no hankies, here," Hilma snapped. "Ve don't even have toilet paper." She floundered toward the door as the fish made one monumental lunge. And, with that rushing line tangled around the legs of the card table, and sent it spinning. The coffee pot and stew kettle crashed and splattered the back of Olga's deerstalker with bits of cabbage and carrot. As the fish resumed his run, the table crashed into the stove, tipping it on its side, spilling fire, which ignited the back wall of the house. The flames rapidly spread to the roof.

"Abandon ship," Olga yelled, and we all scrambled outside. Flames licked the wooden walls of the icehouse.

From a house 10 yards distant, a fisherman burst out and ran toward us, head down against the wind, oblivious to our predicament. "You'll never believe this," he shouted. "All of a sudden I see three-four bobbers come swooping by, and then my line is hit, and I lose my whole rig. Must have been a world record northern." He leaned over and pressed his mittened thumb against one nostril and snorted out snot. "Never seen nothing like that before," he said, before raising his eyes and noticing our fire. "What in the world happened here?"

"Fish," Howard said dejectedly.

"Fish? What do you mean, fish?"

"Mister, you wouldn't believe it anyway," said Olga.

She was no doubt right. Almost nobody else did either, which was a great consternation to Hilma, who told many of her acquaintances at work and friends from church about her experience. "They just don't believe me," she complained several days later. "And Mrs. Grandahl just out and says, 'Hilma, you're a liar.' Imagine, calling me a liar!"

Howard smiled kindly and put his hand on her shoulder. "Now you know what all us fishermen go through," he told her. "If I was to take you to the Friendly Tavern down on Fourth Street and have you tell that story, nobody would call you a liar, Hilma. They'd just say, 'That old lady's a real fisherman.'"

Fishing Angola

KEITH "CATFISH" SUTTON

I never thought I'd go to prison for fishing, but I did. On May 8, 1989, I was processed for entry into the Louisiana State Penitentiary at Angola, a prison known during the late 1960s as "the bloodiest prison in the South," due to the number of inmate assaults.

"Lean against the wall and spread your legs," said one of the heavily armed guards who patted me down. Another guard lay on a mechanic's creeper and pulled himself beneath my truck to search for contraband. Two others were doing a thorough search of everything inside and outside the vehicle. Nothing was left unscrutinized.

Three friends—Lewis Peeler, W.T. Moore, and Curt Moore—were also being processed. I will never forget the looks on their faces as the guards searched them. They looked like condemned men.

"Sir, you'll have to leave this here," one guard said, holding up my camera and film.

"I have Warden Butler's permission to take it inside," I replied.

"I don't think so," he told me. "Photos aren't allowed." Quickly, he dialed a phone. "Give me Warden Butler," he said. A moment of silence passed, then he spoke. "Yes, sir. Yes, sir. I understand."

The guard turned to me, a stern look on his face. "You can take the camera," he said, "but Warden Butler said to remind you the photos you take aren't for publication."

"I understand."

"The four of you can go then," he said. "Park beside the lake, and be sure to lock everything and take the keys with you. And remember, you must leave the prison no later than 5 p.m. If you don't show up on time, you could find yourself here longer than you expected." As he said that, he smiled for the first time.

Thirty minutes later, we were fishing on the prison lake.

A fellow outdoor writer in the Bayou State was the first to tell me about the incredible fishing on Angola's Lake Killarney, when I mentioned to him that my three friends and I had planned a fishing trip that would take us to several Mississippi River oxbow lakes in eastern Louisiana. We intended to fish exclusively for crappie, a beautiful silvery panfish with black spots—often called sac-a-lait, speckled perch, or calico perch. This fish's strike is often so delicate, it may be hooked before you know it. Weighing not much more than a pound or two, crappies put up an admirable tussle on light tackle, but they're not hard fighters. Despite all these things, however, anglers love crappie, which are widespread, abundant and relatively easy to catch. Best of all, crappie are delicious to eat. When fried up golden-delicious, they make a meal fit for a king.

The oxbow lakes along the Mississippi River in Louisiana serve up some of the finest angling for big crappie in the world, and we intended to spend a full week fishing one oxbow one day and another the next until we made our way from Lake Bruin on the north to False River Lake on the south.

"If you like, I can get you permission to fish the best crappie lake in the world," the writer told me. "This is the only lake where I've ever seen an honest-to-god 5-pound crappie, and there are tons of 2- to 3-pounders. You won't be able to do a story about your trip, though. The folks who control access to the lake don't want anyone knowing about the great fishing there, and you have to have connections to get in. Are you interested?"

"Of course, I am," I replied.

"Then I'll talk to the warden and see if I can get you in," he said.

"Warden? Is the lake on a prison or something?" I asked.

"That's right," he said. "It's on the grounds of Angola, the largest maximum-security prison in the United States. That's why you need connections to get in."

"Getting in is not what worries me, then," I told him. "If I go, I just want to be sure you've got connections to get me back *out*."

A week later, Angola warden Hilton Butler called to discuss my visit.

"Lake Killarney is an old oxbow of the Mississippi River," he said, "and because we control access to it and only a few people ever fish there, the crappie grow really big. I like to think of it as *my* lake, and I wouldn't want some nosy writer telling the whole world about the great fishing on Angola prison. So if you want to fish here, you have to assure me you'll never write an article about fishing here as long as I'm the warden."

"I assure you I won't," I said. "But I would like to photograph any big crappie I catch. Would that be okay?"

"I don't suppose that would hurt," he said. "But don't be taking photos of anything else on the prison grounds. Only fish."

He explained the other rules as well. I could bring three friends, and we could use two boats. Fishing was allowed from 8 a.m. to 5 p.m. and we'd have to be processed at the prison gate before we could enter. We couldn't take anything but fishing gear onto the grounds, and we could travel only to and from Lake Killarney. All other parts of the prison were off limits.

Several things about Angola stand out in my mind. I remember seeing gun-toting guards on horseback watching inmates hoeing weeds in the perfect rows of cotton, corn, and other crops. I remember how incredibly beautiful and clean the prison grounds were—at least the part we were permitted to see. The complex of immaculate cellblocks and dormitories is surrounded by eighteen thousand acres of farm fields and perfectly manicured lawns. Even the razor wire lining the miles of fences looked like it had been hand polished.

Some ugly truths were hidden behind that beautiful façade. Angola houses more than five thousand inmates. Ninety percent of those inmates will die there—the average sentence is about eighty-eight years. Angola has more prisoners who will never be released than any other prison in America.

Some call it the Alcatraz of the South. Others call it "The Farm," a title also given to a celebrated 1998 documentary about the prison. Reforms have brought changes for the better, but during much of Angola's more than 100-year history, life was woven by the thread of violence. The only law was that of the knife, and the only protection available to prisoners was what they could acquire through sheer force of character and the ability to impose their will upon others. As prisoner Wilbert Rideau wrote, "The pursuit of survival fueled a heated arms race among the prisoners for the superior weapon: a sword over a knife, a broadax over a sword, and a gun over everything . . . the knife claimed the lives of forty prisoners between 1972 and 1975 and left 350 more seriously injured."

Fishing beneath cypress trees draped in Spanish moss on scenic Lake Killarney, we did not talk about these things. Instead, we focused on fishing. The crappie angling was excellent; a jig dropped near good cover might produce one or a dozen slabs. We did not catch the fabled 5-pounder, or even a 3-pounder, but during two days there, we caught almost fifty crappie in the 2-pound class.

We returned in 1990 and fished Killarney once more. At the time, a new warden was coming on board, and he soon decided to make the lake off-limits to outside anglers. Supposedly, a prisoner had recently hotwired a fisherman's vehicle and tried to drive it through the front gate in an attempted escape. We were the last anglers to drop hooks into the lake.

As the years pass, and the other oxbows of the Mississippi become more fished out, my thoughts can't help but return to Killarney. It's ironic: My three friends and I have spent hours trying to come up with a way back inside those walls, while five thousand criminals sit in their cells plotting any way out. I suppose that any time we put up a fence and lock anybody inside, we're also locking ourselves out.

Getting Spooled

PHILLIP GENTRY

I've always been intrigued by the concept of getting spooled. For the uninitiated, "getting spooled" is a fisherman's slang term for hooking a fish so large and powerful that it strips all the line from the reel despite the reel's drag system and reaches the very end of the line—which hasn't seen daylight since it was tied on. The classic spooling tale ends with the knot tied to the spool giving up the ghost and the fish leaving with all your line. There is an acceptable variation of the tale in which the line breaks somewhere between the spool and the hook. The ultra-classic horror story of spooling involves the fish reaching to the end of the line and jerking the rod out of the boat. I once lost a favorite rod and reel that way while fishing off a public pier at the beach. The reel was still screaming drag as the entire rod went over the side and into the water below, never to be seen again.

As I said, I'm intrigued by the concept. It's not that I don't believe it happens, like sightings of Bigfoot or the Loch Ness monster; it's just that it seems to happen to some people more often than others. It's the ultimate, unverifiable fish tale: "Man, I had one spool me last Saturday. It left out of here and I never could get it turned and it just . . . spooled me." It implies that the spoolee regularly gets on the big fish, but the tackle can't keep up. "Not my fault, I got spooled."

Apart from the aforementioned pier-fishing incident, I have only been spooled one other time, and that was under extenuating circumstances.

This event occurred many years ago during my college days in the coastal city of Charleston, South Carolina. A buddy of mine—who shall remain nameless—and I had the grand idea, one late summer evening, to do a little night fishing from the bridge that crossed the inlet between two of the coastal islands near where we went to school. Back in those days we didn't pay much attention to tides or what fish were biting, and most of our excursions involved bottom fishing with frozen shrimp.

We set up on the catwalk alongside the bridge and dutifully cast our lines as far as possible out into the vast reaches of the inlet. My buddy was fishing with a huge 9-and-a-half-foot surf rod that could have doubled as a pool cue and a likewise monstrous spinning reel that would have held a thousand yards of 10- or 15-pound test-line if he hadn't spooled it with cheap 60-pound high-test super-mono from the discount store. With lines out we commenced happy hour, which was the main reason for the trip in the first place, and monitored the traffic passing less than 5 feet behind us for college girls returning from an afternoon on the beach.

Soon our beer cooler was much lighter and my buddy decided he'd walk to the bait shop at the other end of the bridge and re-supply. He asked if I'd watch his rod while he was gone. "Sure, no problem," I offered absently.

As soon as College Buddy was out of sight, the rod tip on the old pool cue began twitching. I eyed the rod for several seconds and determined that something alive was indeed connected with the other end of the line. If I could time the set just right I could get the hook into the fish before he stole the bait.

As I said, we didn't pay much attention to tides in those days and it so happened that the tide was going out—pretty strongly, as a matter of fact. I was mistaken in thinking that College Buddy had a bite. In reality, his fishing rig, a 1-ounce weight with a small Styrofoam float to keep the bait off the bottom, had lost its fight with the tide and, instead of lying dutifully on the bottom, was bobbing on the surface some distance away at the very end of the line.

But I had yet to realize this while standing on that bridge, doubled-

over, rod in hand, about to do my imitation of Roland Martin with a
pool cue. In addition to fishing, College Buddy and I shared a love of
hitting the weight pile at the school gym, followed by additional reps of
12-ounce curls once we left the gym. Both of us were pretty low-key, but
we each stood better than 6 feet tall and weighed over 200 pounds. We
were the kind of Southern boys that co-eds called up when they wanted
something moved, like a couch up five flights of stairs or a refrigerator
from one apartment to another.

It would take a team of engineers to calculate the exact velocity
achieved by a 1-ounce weight when an exuberant 200-pound college
male leverages 9-and-a-half feet of fiberglass against it like a catapult.
Suffice it to say that the weight came back at me as if it had been shot
from a muzzleloader. It zipped past my head so close that I could actually smell the stench of rotting shrimp trailing on the hook behind the
speeding projectile before it clanged into the bridge structure behind
me.

There was a moment of joy and ecstasy in the realization that I'd
just done something incredibly stupid and lived to tell about it. Not
only lived, but I didn't have a scratch on me. That moment was shattered
an instant later when a second realization struck: the projectile weight
had not banged into the bridge structure behind me but had somehow
lodged in the front grill of a Volkswagen bus, one of the many that fer-
ried back and forth from the beach in those days.

Still gripping the rod from my forceful attempt at sinking the hook
deep into Moby Fish, I was suddenly spun 270 degrees and faced in the
direction of the retreating bus. The scream of the monster reel's drag
was deafening. Instinct told me to hang on to the rod. After all, it wasn't
even mine, and I had been put in charge of watching it. Within seconds
the VW bus, oblivious to the lead weight and piece of rotting crustacean
stuck in its grill, reached the maximum distance allowed by the spool of
60-pound mono. I was spooled!

With a loud crack the line parted company, leaving only a 10-yard
strand of stretched nylon clinging to the reel as I cart-wheeled from the
intense recoil of the catapult in my shaking hands. Barely avoiding a
back flip off the inlet bridge, I slumped into my seat beside the railing.

Still shell-shocked, I laid the rod back down against the bridge railing, the spent shred of line trailing off with the tide. Fifteen minutes or two hours later, I'm still not sure which, College Buddy returned to the scene and asked if there'd been any action. I just nodded my head no. He reeled in his line and discovered only 10 yards of line left, then asked me what happened.

"Don't know," I replied. "A shark must have swum by and bit it off."

"A shark?" He was incredulous.

"What do you think happened?" I poured on the sarcasm. "The big one came along and spooled that 60-pound high-test super-mono? Without me even noticing? C'mon, buddy. It would take a fish the size of a bus to do something like that." It was all I could do to keep a straight face.

College buddy shrugged and cracked open another beer.

To this day I've never told him what actually occurred that night on the bridge. Who would ever believe I got spooled by a Volkswagen?

A Manly Sport

JOHN MEDEIROS

I admit it. I'm a man of contradictions. I despise McDonald's and the globalization of fast-food culture, but at the same time I'm ready to argue that the Egg McMuffin is quite possibly the Eighth Wonder of the world. Though I generally frown upon the use of alcohol, I simply love the way it makes me feel. So it is no wonder that I, a gay man who never understood the concept behind hunting or competitive sports, enjoy the mysteries of fishing. Some of my friends tell me they think fishing is an anti-social activity—but then again, so is masturbation, and you don't find them abstaining from that. Actually, for me, the two are pretty similar. If you think about it, fishing is nothing more than a guy sitting on a dock with his pole in his hand waiting for it to be yanked.

Because I love fishing so much (not to mention masturbation), I make it a point every year to do it as much as I possibly can. When March first comes around, I'm among the avid Minnesota pole-holders eagerly waiting in line to purchase their annual fishing license. Even though I normally don't start fishing until June or July, there is satisfaction in knowing that I have the freedom to whip out my pole whenever I want to.

Buying a license is an artistic talent for a gay man. It is not simply a matter of going to the store and making your purchase, as if it were a loaf of bread or fresh quiche from the deli. Oh, no. One must be properly dressed for the occasion. I employ the "New England guy look"—blue jeans, a white tee-shirt, red flannel shirt (unbuttoned) and beige construction boots. Whenever I wear this outfit, my partner knows I am either on my way to buy my fishing license, or the Eagle (our local gay bar) is having one of its dress-code nights.

When buying a license, it helps to have your hair a bit disheveled, and one should avoid shaving at all costs. I once made the mistake of buying a license on my way home from a friend's wedding. With the sales person still laughing at me, I managed to convince him that I was visiting from Iowa and bought a non-resident weekend license instead. Tuxedos and bait shops mix about as well as Viagra and sleeping pills.

And where you buy your license makes a difference. I prefer the bait and tackle shops located an hour outside of the city, where folks say things like, "You betcha" through stained teeth. They don't bother looking up when you make your purchase. Otherwise, any sporting goods store will do.

For me the goal of fishing is the action—or inaction—itself. It's knowing that when I fish, I am living the contradiction. Fishing is never about the catch—at least, that's what I thought, until the day that made me stop fishing for good.

It's mid-May. Fishing opener in Minnesota. My partner, Steve, and I are vacationing at a friend's cabin in northern Wisconsin. To say it is quiet here is an understatement. This is the kind of place that echoes each sound you make, where a sneeze sends a flock of heron a hundred yards away flying off into the distance. It's 2 p.m. or so, and we have spent the last thirty minutes catching guppy-sized teasers, not big enough to use as bait, much less keep for dinner. Steve's mom, Rose, is sitting on the dock with us, along with her sister, Barb, who takes a moment to look up from her book to say to me, "John, you got a bite der."

Sure enough, my bobber is twitching, and I reel in a 6-inch sunny. Not a bad size; definitely worth keeping. Finally, I think to myself, we're going to catch some keepers.

Steve's Aunt Barb is a no-nonsense type of gal who speaks with a dry wit. She grew up on a farm in rural Minnesota. Unlike me she isn't afraid of wasps, or bats, or badly cooked meat. She sees my catch and makes her way to my tackle box where she casually retrieves the stringer. As any good fisherman knows, to use the stringer correctly you insert the spear through the fish's gill, then through the mouth, and then through the metal ring at the end. You then put the fish back in the water, and tie your stringer to the dock, which is exactly what Barb does without flinching. I immediately re-bait my hook and cast it out again, ready for my next big catch. Steve casts his line close to mine, since we now know where the fish are biting. And we wait.

And wait.

Nothing.

It's odd to catch one sunfish without catching several, and by now, we've been waiting about twenty minutes. And while we wait, I look down at my stringer only to find it bobbing up and down like a teenager at a rock concert. "Your sunny looks like he's having a party down der," says Barb. "You might want to find out what he's up to."

I grab the stringer and pull up the fish and notice that my catch has gotten considerably heavier. "Holy crap," I yell. "Something's got a bite on my sunny!" I'm wondering what I might pull up. Would I even be able to tell? As I'm thinking all this, I yank the string, and whatever is down there fights me for just a few seconds before releasing its grip, and I pull my sunfish out of the water.

It is mangled—its tail has been savagely ripped from its body. And whatever cannibal is eating away at my fish is directly below us, under this dock . . .

"Oh, my God! Get a look at this . . . what is it?" I start freaking out. "What the heck is down there?"

"You might have a Northern down der," says Barb. "I bet dat's what you got."

"But what the hell do I do now?" I shout, sending off a flock of geese two counties away.

"Well, you can still keep your sunfish, looks like only the tail's gone. Dat is, if you want it." It's hard to tell if Barb is joking or not, but I'm not about to dine on anything that looks like Jeffrey Dahmer just spat it out.

Steve rolls his eyes and says, "Oh, John, it's just a fish. Put the sunfish back in the water and when the cannibal bites again, I'll pull him in. Don't be such a wuss." So I, in my wussiest fashion, gently place the sunfish back in the water, watching with the anticipation of a frightened child. I study the water and follow its swirl as whatever is left of my sunfish circles its way to the bottom. And sure enough, before the water has had a chance to still itself, a bubble like a small mushroom cloud emerges to the surface, and in no time the monster below once again goes after my beautiful 6-inch catch.

Steve is one of those strong and muscular gay men, but without the attitude, a contradiction in his own right. Though 14 years my senior, at 52 he can pin me down in one count. So to see him struggle to lift this beast out of the water means only one thing—that it is bigger and stronger than any of us thought. Nevertheless, Steve pulls up the catch, and as it makes its way out of the water we stand in awe.

"Holy crap!" I shriek in a near-banshee squeal. "Look at the size of that thing!"

Flashback to 1965. The year of my birth was characterized by three significant events: (1) the first U.S. combat troops arrived in Vietnam; (2) black nationalist leader Malcolm X was shot to death in Harlem; and (3) *Gamera the Invincible* was released in the United States. For those who don't remember the movie, noted zoologist Eiji Hidaka and his lady assistant Kyoko visit the North Pole to investigate the possible modern-day whereabouts of the lost continent of Atlantis. While they are there, an aircraft equipped with nuclear weapons is shot down, awakening a giant prehistoric, fire-breathing, saber-tusked turtle monster named Gamera.

I bring this to your attention because at this point in the story, my sunfish and I just caught Gamera.

I stand in shock. Dangling before me with my sunfish in its mouth, is the largest snapping turtle I have ever seen in my life. Its body is the size of my entire torso, and I soon find myself dancing the Dance of Fear, formerly performed only by Curly Howard of the Three Stooges and certain cartoon characters. It starts with my feet tapping uncontrollably, running in place without actually going anywhere, and ends with my hands hysterically flailing above my head while I run around in circles shrieking "Omigod! Omigod!" as I try desperately to catch my breath between gasps of air.

Barb and Rose, on the other hand, are cool as cucumbers. They're calmly sitting on the dock bench, politely ignoring me—or perhaps not even noticing my flailing—while they try to recall their recipes for turtle soup. "Oh, I like to cut my turtle meat up into little bits," says Barb. "Dat way the kids'll eat it."

And Steve sneers, with the patience and arrogance of a Webelos cub scout master, as he hauls up the catch. "John" he says to me, "Get it by the neck, but be careful! It can bite your finger clean off. In fact, even if you chop the head off and put it in a bucket, it can still bite off your finger— even after seven days!"

Seven days, I think to myself. A head, in a bucket, still hungry and able to eat me even after seven days . . . this is the stuff nightmares are made of.

Gamera then looks me dead in the eye, as if knowing that I am the only one he is frightening, and releases his grip on the sunfish, plunging back into the depths from where he came.

By now my sunfish is nothing more than a head attached to a piece of string.

I take no more risks and run up the stairs toward the cabin, which only means something once you know that there are about seventy-five steps and I climb them in five seconds flat. My heart is racing as if I'd just faced the Devil himself. Steve and his family point at me and laugh, and say they've never had so much fun catching a snapping turtle before. "What ya doing all the way up there, honey?" Steve asks with a chuckle. "Come back down and help us catch some more fish."

The three of them have the exact same laugh. It's like a high pitched cackle with a little bit of schoolyard bully thrown in for effect. These people are not of this planet, I tell myself. They are doing this all wrong. They are supposed to run for their lives and throw their hands over their heads like they do in the Japanese movies. They're supposed to scream. Why aren't they screaming? Instead they are conjuring up recipes for amphibian stew.

It's no use explaining my reaction. Their skin is much thicker than that. They are native Minnesotans. Their outer shells are as hard as Gamera's.

I've haven't fished since that encounter with terror. Fishing is supposed to be about relaxation, about living the gay contradiction. It is not supposed to be about monsters lurking in murky water.

I'm looking for a new hobby. In the meantime, I've reverted to the other kind of pole-holding. It's antisocial, I know—but at least I know what to expect.

The Summer of *Jaws*

KATHLEEN GERARD

When you share a fishing rod with your brother, the phrase *Either fish or cut bait* has literal significance. That was the order of things in the summer of 1975, when our family spent two weeks in late August vacationing on Cape Cod. My brother, thirteen to my eleven years, got first dibs on the fishing pole. That left me to cut squid with a rusty old pocket knife atop our father's tackle box—a steel army-surplus box labeled "ammunition."

Good things come to those who bait was my favorite expression that summer. We prided ourselves on being a family of annual anglers. There was the summer of 1971, where in one week, my big sisters each caught an eel—one 4-foot, one almost 6—right off the pier where I set up our crab traps in Beach Haven, New Jersey. In 1973, the blowfish in the North Atlantic were so plentiful they practically jumped into our small boat and one day, when we caught over two hundred, nearly capsized it. But the most notable occurrence during those years was my father's four-hour-long battle on the North Carolina shore. He puffed on a cigar, stood thigh-high in the surf, and reeled on a heavily bent rod. After the prolonged struggle, a 40-pound, 10-foot wide stingray emerged from the surf.

"Let him make someone else's memory," my father said, taking a quick picture of the ray flailing in the sand. He cut the line and dragged the creature back into the surf, where it flapped back to deeper waters.

But fishing in my family was always more about the mythology than about the act in itself. Perhaps because our parents were both educators, baiting hooks and casting lines was inseparable from critical discussions of Hemingway's *The Old Man and The Sea*, or captains Ahab and Nemo. The ocean was a place where, above all, one's imagination was able to swim freely. And imagination was something that ran wildly overactive in my brother and me during those two weeks we spent on Cape Cod in 1975.

It was the summer of *Jaws*. I'd read and re-read the book by Peter Benchley, the first grown-up bestseller I'd undertaken. And then I'd seen the movie by Steven Spielberg three times in theaters with my brother, Tom. An obsessive imitator, Tom nailed Robert Shaw's bombastic, obsessed shark-hunter Quint down to his accent. He would borrow my aviator-shaped eyeglasses to do stunning imitations of Roy Schneider, who played the chief of police haunted by the great white as it terrorized his Long Island beach town.

My stomach hurt from laughing as Tom perfected his impersonations and re-enactments of big scenes from the movie. And he was in rarer-than-rare form the day he and I set out on Cape Cod Bay in a tiny rowboat fitted with an outboard motor—the smallest one they had for rent at the dock, the only one we could afford as we exchanged our money for a shared seafaring dream.

We were giddy with excitement. We'd gotten permission from our parents to take our first solo fishing expedition. Before we left, Dad went over the nuances of the outboard motor. Tom and I mentally rolled our eyes as both our parents sat us down and gave us a lecture about responsibility, safety, life jackets, and our limits (the bay only—we were not to drift out into the ocean).

My brother and I had enough money to test our skills at sea for four hours. We brought along lunch, bait, tackle, our shared fishing pole, suntan lotion, and a paperback copy of *Jaws*. We set out on a clear, bright morning into the calm still of Cape Cod Bay.

My brother drove and I gleefully played first mate to his captain. I sat at the bow, while Tom throttled up the outboard motor. The little boat's nose lifted in the air and the wind pushed on our faces. In the distance I watched hang-gliders skimming off the dunes. About a mile out into the bay, we could still see the rounded hook of Provincetown, the very tip of the Cape. Soon Tom cut the engine. He cast our line and we let ourselves drift.

I was used to fishing with the whole family, mostly on docks or piers. To be so far from land in such a tiny boat with only my brother felt eerie. The calm waters seemed menacing and threatening without my parents' presence. And when I looked over the side of the boat, the water seemed especially dark and abysmal.

Not wanting to give voice to my fears, I sucked in a deep breath of salty air then dangled my legs over the edge of the boat. I spent much of the late morning with my feet in the water. Tom and I ate lunch, read passages from *Jaws*, and waited for something to bite our line. The pole was anchored in a stirrup on the side of the boat. We both watched it obsessively. During the wait, my brother lifted my glasses from my face, put them on his own, and slipped into his Chief Brody impersonation. He did the scene from the movie where Brody is given the task of laying a chum line while the crew is at sea, and while he's doing so the enormous shark suddenly looms up behind the boat. Horrified by the sight of it, the panicked Brody announces the shark's presence in a deadpan voice: "You're gonna need a bigger boat!"

The off-shore breeze pushing through our hair should have tipped us off, but it wasn't until we drifted close to shore that we realized the tide or the wind had us in its clutch. We found ourselves wobbling amid some buoys and poles near nets laid by commercial fishing boats. I was unfazed, engrossed in re-reading *Jaws*, and sunning myself. My bare feet were kicking into the water when my brother decided we'd better get ourselves moving again.

The pull-start on the outboard was turning the motor, but not starting it. As hard as he tried—fiddling over and over again with the throttle and shift lever—my brother couldn't get the engine going.

While Tom was trying to get us back in transit, the tip of our fishing pole suddenly arched way down into the water. As I turned my attention to the pole, my brother said, "Kath, don't turn around. Just get your feet out of the water and into the boat." His voice was even and steady.

"Look," I exclaimed, pointing to the pole. The stirrup to which it was anchored moaned under the immensity of the pull. "We've got a big one!"

"Kath. Do what I'm telling you." Urgency laced his tone. "Don't move too fast or splash, just get your feet into the boat."

"But . . ."

"Feet. Boat. Now."

I did as he commanded, and when I turned and followed the gaze of his wide eyes, I saw the dark rise of a fin cutting through the water, heading straight for us. I scurried to the center of the boat, making it wobble furiously.

The bay went silent as Tom and I aimed our sights on the sleek triangular fin that stood two feet out of the water. The fin moved alongside the boat, in arms reach. Then it circled us. The anterior of the fin was jagged like a serrated knife. I sat there, mouth unhinged, staring past the fin at the murky outline of the body attached to it. The shark was the length of our boat.

OhmyGod! We're gonna die! I thought, as my palms sweated and my stomach roiled. I couldn't take my unblinking eyes off the water. I kept searching for that fin. *Where did it go? Was it under us? And what if there was more than one shark under there?* Shivering, I jerked my bare, wet feet up from the floor of the boat and hugged my knees to my chest atop the slab of the seat.

Our fishing pole doubled over and the stirrup moaned. The shark re-emerged, circling, prowling the water around us. Was he searching for a meal near the fishing nets?

My brother was still pulling on the start cord. Finally he leaned over the stern and reached into the water. "What are you doing? Are you crazy?" I shrieked.

"There's something wrapped around the propeller. I've got to untangle it." Sweat poured off his face as he pulled long strands of seaweed away from the propeller along with fishing line. But when he'd freed things enough, he gave the starter cord a pull so fierce that it not only jump-started the engine, but the nose of the boat jerked high in the air and our fishing rod popped out of the stirrup. Our pole and reel soared like a javelin out into the bay and sank. My brother watched silently.

He cranked the motor to full throttle, and we raced back to the dock—even though we had two hours left on our rental.

For the rest of our vacation my brother made no more impersonations of fictional characters being scared by a shark. It wasn't funny anymore. I've seen the movie a few times since, but now *Jaws* looks like exactly what it was: a composite of several crude and malfunctioning robots. It's no match in terror for the real thing.

Not the Best Fishing Hole

LEN RICH

During the 1990s I built and operated a sport-fishing camp in the Labrador wilderness. As the host, I had to treat my guests with a bit more diplomacy and sensitivity than I would my normal fishing buddies. There were times when I had to bite my tongue to keep from laughing out loud at the antics of the tourists/fishermen who kept me in business.

One of my guests, let's call him Fred, got into the sauce one evening after supper and took in a little more than his system could handle. He mixed himself several rum-and-cokes, heavy on the rum and light on the coke. After an hour or so, his speech grew thick, and he had some trouble navigating. I figured that since it was his vacation, he had the right to cut loose a little.

Soon Fred arose from the table and went outside, then staggered along the trail to the outhouse. In short time, my staff and I heard him retching. Discretion being the better part of valor, we left him alone to clean out his system. For my part, I was relieved that, given his condition, he'd at least found the makeshift toilet.

It was quiet for a while, then footsteps came back along the boardwalk, sort of shuffling. I heard Fred mumbling under his breath. He passed by the window, disappeared for a few minutes then returned with his fishing rod, heading back to the outhouse. Curiosity and a sense of responsibility got the better of me, so I followed to see where he was going with that fly rod. When I rounded the corner I spotted Fred half hanging out of the privy, his head close to the hole of the toilet seat, dipping his line up and down.

"Hey, Fred, you aren't going to catch any fish in there!" I yelled, and he straightened up in a hurry, startled by my voice.

"I know, I know." Something was wrong with his speech. "It's my lower denture plate. I threw it up with my supper and that rum. It's sitting on top of the pile, and I'm trying to hook it with the fly!"

Despite my efforts at professionalism, I laughed. The more I thought about it, the funnier it got. Tears were soon flowing down my cheeks at the poor guy's predicament.

"Oh, damn," he mumbled. "It slipped. Now what can I do?"

I asked him to move out of the way and peered into the darkness. There it was, sitting precariously on top of the pile of vomit, human feces, and toilet paper—an expensive piece of dental work.

While Fred recovered his senses, I gathered some of the staff to come and help. We tipped the outhouse onto its side and held it there while Fred lay on his stomach and reached into the mess to retrieve his lower denture. One of the guides held him by his belt as he stretched, and Fred was finally able to get his fingers on it.

He was happy to have it back. We insisted that he wash it thoroughly before its next use. One of the guides suggested we erect a sign next to the toilet seat that said "Fred's Fishing Hole." I had to draw the line there.

Fred didn't touch any more of the hard stuff for the rest of the week, and looked rather sheepish when he came into dinner each night. I made it clear to my employees that they weren't to say anymore about the incident, to spare Fred further embarrassment. But looking back, I can't help but smile at the time one of my guests, in the middle of the Labrador wilderness, went fly fishing in an outhouse.

Hook, Line, and Sinker

BOB BURT

Amputation is not an uncommon situation on commercial fishing boats. Cables snap, steel doors slam, and machinery designed to parse the flesh of fish does not discriminate against skin. With seasons short and expectations high, my leg may become chum before this boat stops fishing.

Outside my portal a snowcapped volcano emerges from a steel gray dawn. Even the sun doesn't like coming this far north. Swirling snow, under the glow of lights from the transom, masquerades as moths, a mirage to tempt the hundreds of hungry seabirds which follow us day after day.

The boat lists; a wave larger than a drive-in movie screen sends my nurse waddling between bunks. Boom! The anchor slams the hull. A wake-up call from the Bering Sea; when it raises, nobody sleeps.

"That was a big 'un," Carla says. She digs into her medical bag. "This will only make you stronger." She draws nectar of mold into a syringe. "Roll over."

Amoxicillin, chilly as the blue water upon which we sail, floods my fatty tissue.

"No good deed ever goes unpunished," I wince, reflecting on the reason for this remedy. Fish scales and dandruff flurry as I nestle back beneath my sleeping bag. It is lumpy and tired. Three years of salt, rust, and diesel have exhausted a billowy spirit.

Mocking the Tooth Fairy, Carla slides a tiny envelope with big Ibuprofens under my pillow.

"Knowledge is power." A finger with an engagement ring taps my forehead. "If you drink that hooch you guys have hidden around here and eat these, your liver will turn to Jell-O. Let me have another look at your piggers." She rolls back the bottom of my sleeping bag and stares at my distended digits. "Ridiculous."

My foot is absurd: swollen to the point of splitting and the color of a manic depressive's mood ring.

"It looks worse than it feels," I say. It feels like humming sand.

Carla's maternal eyes peer over rounded bifocals, the cap of a black marker twists in her teeth and a painted nail follows a red squiggle up from my ankle. "You're growing," she says dashing the end of its trail.

The growth is death. My veins are collapsing. "The wrath of a million dead fish," I sigh. Cellulitis, a staph infection, has gained purchase in my foot; inch by inch, it creeps ever closer toward my heart.

Just below my kneecap Carla etches *Finish Line*. "You're finished if it comes this far," she says. "Your leg is mine."

On a factory trawler, deck positions don't come easy or often, so when a set of weight chains—two kinks of links the size of a Chevy Nova—rolled over a deckhand named Thor and turned his leg into the spongy center of a hard plaster cast, the spot he left on deck opened up for anyone willing to take the bait.

"Are you going for it?" John asks me. Like me John is a processor, part of the human machine that helps this ship digest 30 tons of fish an hour. "Move up and the only time we'll see you is at the incinerator." Greenhorn deck hands are always initiated with trash detail.

For five seasons I have slept above, worked next to, and shared three meals a day with John. We trade music, tales of woe, dirty jokes and hard candy. I've petted his dog, hugged his mother, and wrecked his truck. He's given me athlete's foot, a motorcycle that doesn't work, and the complete works of Nelson Algren. I owe him $370.

John is content in the factory; he'll load freezers, pull roe sacks from an endless gutter of entrails and slam frozen fish into boxes until he can't do it any more, which could be tomorrow or ten years from now.

I look him straight in the eye, something easy to do since he has no eyebrows; he lost them in a poker game after our last off-load. "I'm tired of being a cog in this floating fish holocaust," I tell him. The factory is a cat's cradle of stainless steel, florescent lights, and food-grade plastic designed to morph piscine into protein. "What more can the factory teach me?" I lament the level learning curve. "It's all re-runs from here on out. Carpal tunnel is inevitable. We've done it all. It's time. At least on deck there's daylight, dignity, and some sort of financial future."

John pulls off his hairnet and a crudely carved Mohawk tells me he's been playing poker again. He changes the subject. "Wanna do Rock, Paper, Scissors to see who has to break up the piles in the live tanks?"

Live tanks is the industry term for the compartment on a fishing boat that circulates ocean water where the catch can be loaded and brought to shore alive. In our boat there's no water in the live tank. It's a place the size of a six-car garage where fish are dropped to die. The only way in is through a hydraulic door; out is by someone's mercy.

"Captain on the boat says shoot," I say as I throw my hand sign for scissors. The piles are mounds of deceased fish locked together by decay. Their once slippery scales are now like glue, and they won't make it into the factory unless someone takes boots, a shovel, and a fire hose to them.

"Rock breaks scissors," John pounds my peace sign.

In the live tank the ceiling drips. Rust blooms on the welds of the walls. It's dark, dank, and surprisingly peaceful. The rest of the ship is bathed in mayhem but in this tomb there's solitude; no one to talk to except the lump sucker that rolls like a half-filled water balloon between my bent shovel and the flattened chandelier that used to be a jellyfish. Lump suckers are fat and scaleless, dead ringers for Ronald McDonald's friend, Grimace. They have an adhesive disk on their chin and for kicks we stick them to the ceiling where they'll hang like a blubbery speed-bag for the next four hours. My gloved fingers reach for an I-beam from which to hang it.

I begin kicking apart the pile of dead fish. If I'm successful they'll flow out into the factory where they'll be decapitated, eviscerated, skinned, and filleted. Their flesh will be mixed in an auger with sugar and bovine plasma until it becomes surimi: the principal component of fish sticks and imitation crab.

"Haul back!" The deck boss's voice echoes through the PA. This is my invitation to audition on deck.

"John!" I holler. "This is it, let me out!" Hauling back means bringing in a net big enough to snare a 747. "John! Let me out!"

His lips press the scratched and scaly glass. "Shame if you're still in there and they dump that bag." His speech is double-muddled by a dip in his lip and a butterscotch candy on his tongue.

If they dump the net I'll spend the next three hours clawing the ceiling with the Lump Sucker, testing a floor made of ten thousand squirming foot-long fish. "Let me out," I beg.

"Got gloves?" He asks. The smile of power, the lever to lift the doors is within his reach.

"I swear on the electrical tape I wrap around my rubber pants if you..." I can see the salt water rash on his wrists so I know he's desperate. "Let me out and I'll have two new rights in your locker by the end of the shift." Gloves without holes are worth more than gold this late in the season. Our shift's end is more than sixteen hours away, plenty of time to welch on my offer or trip him up with a double or nothing. "Open the goddamn door. I'm too old for this shit. I want my sea time to be worth something. I want my AB"—AB is the able-bodied seaman credential, the first rung on the long ladder that climbs to the rank of captain—"I could work tugs ... ferries ... research vessels ... two weeks on and two weeks off; three months on and two months off. I could get benefits. I want choices, John. I got carpal tunnel, no feeling in two toes from frostbite, scars galore, and a venereal disease; I'm ready to graduate from processor to fisherman. Open the door."

I spill out into the trough with four hundred dead Pollock. "Don't fuck up," John says.

I run with my hard hat and life jacket into a wind that whips white off the waves. For the first time in a month I can see the horizon. "I'm here," I announce.

Hands sheathed in rubber play the net like a harp while cigarettes dangle and winches whine. The deck crew is not impressed by my presence; they are a band of brothers held together by work, gusto, and sexual harassment. They've been together so long they no longer have to speak unless it's about sodomy, trucks, or the stock market.

"I want in," I say, staking out Thor's spot.

The deck boss's stare is as cold as the wind in the wires. His head nods.

I join in the untying of the cod end, the mesh casing where the net funnels the fish. It is 8 feet high, 40 feet long and packed with gaping mouths. A million little eyes watch as the orange line splays with a touch of my knife.

"Look," I say pointing out a fish that's not like the others, "a brownie!"

Pollock, our target fish, is the largest biomass on earth next to insects. They can school a mile wide and a hundred feet deep. A brownie is a rock fish protected by Endangered Species Act. I pick up the protected one from the pollock. "Breathe!" I say to it.

"Leave it," the deck boss grunts. "Let it be."

"Use your gills!" I ignore the boss and the jibes of the deck crew. "Choose life!" As I'm about to toss him overboard I stumble over a hook the size of my head and fumble the fish. Brownies have spines in their dorsal fins sharp enough to puncture a neoprene boot and this one is no exception. When the fish falls its fin finds my foot. "Mother of pearl . . . " I shriek. It flips and flops until it tumbles down the stern ramp where the propeller turns it into bloody jetsam.

"Sometimes it takes a hook to straighten people out," the Deck Boss says. "I say leave it, you leave it." Fists and insults fly on fishing boats, excuses don't. "Go back down to the factory." Smoke swirls from his chapped lips. "Don't call us, we'll call you."

At the hatch I stop and look back. A gray blanket of clouds has lain low over the sea. The horizon is gone. The only thing I have to navigate by is a wake peppered with the flesh of my mistake.

"Who would think dorsal fins are an incubator for all things toxic?" I question Carla. My puncture wound bloomed not long after my feet hit the factory floor; by shift's end the swelling inside my boot displaced my disappointment over the deck job.

Carla straps on her stethoscope but no instrument of amplification is necessary to hear the unusual explosion that suddenly comes from inside my bathroom.

"That's a new noise," Carla says.

The stateroom I share with five others sandwiches a bathroom with another room. That other room is known as "Little Vietnam." Six brothers, all from Southeast Asia, bunk there. They smoke more than a tire incinerator. They listen to Cliff Richard. And they cook rice in the shower stall.

The door to head opens, out shuffles Dung, the second oldest brother. "Bob," he says to me, his pants are around his ankles and poop is plastered to his legs, chest, and chin. "What the fuck?" It is the first time I've heard him speak English.

"Just when I thought I'd seen it all," Carla says.

"Dung," I point skyward to his silhouette stenciled by scat, "you're on the ceiling." Nothing I've ever said has been so true.

"It's that goddamn Wayne," Carla curses the assistant engineer. "He said at breakfast, 'If anyone flushes anymore shit down the toilet that ain't shit, I swear, from my lips to God's ear, I'll reverse the vacuum hoses and blow a hundred pounds of air up the pipes.'" Her impression of Wayne is spot on; she even holds a comb under her nose to mimic his walrus mustache. "Somebody should have given that boy more hugs when he was a baby," she remarks. "Dung, honey. Take a shower, you're making me sick."

Her palm pumps a ball as a cuff squeezes my arm. "Shane's eye was worse," Carla places my pain in a pecking order. "The Coast Guard picked him up. They ended up using Q-tips and diesel to get his eye open." Shane caught a glob of glue in the face. It was heated to 300 degrees and affixed his eyelid to his eyeball. "At least he got to go home early."

My calluses peel petals of pale flesh—the fruit of moist heat. "Shane's home is a van on 41st Street in Seattle," I remind her. I eat a horse pill and chase it with water that tastes exactly like the pipe from which it was poured. "I was so close to getting on deck, Carla, so close." Reality hurts more than my malady. "Stupid endangered species. I'll say it again, no good deed ever goes unpunished."

Carla shakes her head. "Isn't there something else you could be doing?" My surrogate mother sounds a lot like my real mother, whom lo-gistics allow only one phone call a month.

Those are strained conversations. The pay phones of Dutch Harbor, Alaska carry conversation to the lower 48 through a satellite connection, it takes a full second for words to wander that far, and it's easy to hear disappointment in the lull.

"I'm praying for you," my mom always says.

The line at the docks for the phone is always ten deep. Calling cards tap gloved hands. Cigarettes puff. Feet shuffle. Everyone wants to throw a line to the outside world.

"This is my religion," I tell her. "The Bering Sea is as much monastery as it is prison."

I was born and raised in the parish of St. John Fisher. How it is lost on my mother that I chose to follow the profession of the patron saint whose portrait I faced week after week is beyond me.

"John was one of the original apostles," I tell Carla now. "He was a fisherman. It's his head that rests on Jesus's breast at the Last Supper." I suck ginger ale through a straw. "He never left his side, not when they ar-rested him, jailed, tried, or crucified him. When they spilled Portuguese wine into his pierced side, it dripped on John. Fishing people are like that. They're also like the ocean; the deeper you go, the weirder things get."

Carla packs away her medical wares. "Yeah, well most fishermen are running *from* than *to* somewhere. As much as they're thinking about their wives and girlfriends, they're thinking about what they're going to drink before they see them." A snap shuts her case.

It's an argument I can't refute. "Any mail?" Our ship's nurse is also the post office, galley help, ship's store, laundry, and wake-up service.

"None for you." She enjoys the monthly chore of delivering mail; let-ters written in crayon bring tears to even the meanest of men. "Get some sleep," she smiles, "imitation crab isn't worth losing a limb over."

Contributors

BURKHARD BILGER has been a staff writer at *The New Yorker* since 2000. His articles have appeared in *The Atlantic Monthly, Harper's, The New York Times,* and numerous other publications, and have been anthologized in *The Best American Science and Nature Writing, The Best American Food Writing,* and *The Best American Sports Writing.* His book, *Noodling for Flatheads,* was a finalist for a PEN-Faulkner Award in 2000. Bilger lives in Brooklyn with his wife, Jennifer Nelson, and children, Hans, Ruby, and Evangeline.

BOB BURT spent seven seasons on the *F/V Island Enterprise,* taming the world's appetite for fish sticks. He lives in the Pacific Northwest, where his fish stories get larger every year. He's been writing a novel for fifteen years, and if he ever finishes it, his wife will find other things for him to do.

Born in Chicago, **GENE CABOT** left at seventeen to join the Navy and later traveled for an aircraft modification company. In 1958 he went to the Atlantic Missile Test Range (Cape Canaveral) in Florida and worked on missile-tracking radars on many islands in the Caribbean, Ascension Island, and Greenland. Retired in Panama City, he fishes in lakes and the Gulf of Mexico. His goal is to catch a 30-pound kingfish.

IAN CARD and his father Alan operate the *Challenger,* a 40-foot marlin and tuna charter boat out of Bermuda. He has 20 years' experience in the charter boat business and holds the Bermuda record for catching the largest Mako shark (821 lbs.).

SCOTT CARRIER is a writer and radio producer who lives in Salt Lake City, Utah. His written work has been published in *Esquire, GQ, Rolling Stone, Harper's,* and *Mother Jones* magazines. His story collection, *Running After Antelope,* was published by Counterpoint Press in 2001. His radio stories have been featured on *All Things Considered, This American Life, Marketplace, Day to Day,* and other public radio programs in the United States, Australia, and Canada. He is currently a senior producer for the new NPR weekly series, *Hearing Voices,* and a professor in the Communication Department at Utah Valley University in Orem, Utah.

LAURAN DERIGNE is a writer and high school librarian in St. Louis, Missouri. She enjoys camping, hiking, kayaking and, occasionally, fishing, with her husband, Garret, and their two-year-old son, Sawyer.

As a full-time freelance writer and with monthly columns in *Outdoor Florida Magazine,* **BOB T. EPSTEIN** has spent the past twenty-five years creating and selling articles for hundreds of markets in the U.S and Europe as well as having spent nineteen years as PR Consultant to Olympus Consumer Digital Cameras Corporation. Bob was past president and CEO of the sixty-year-old Florida Outdoor Writers Association. Bob has been a Scripps Howard News Service freelancer and specials writer for *Treasure Coast* Newspapers. Bob is a columnist for Frederick, Maryland daily newspaper titled *Frederick News-Post* food section, and freelances for their travel section, additionally he contributed a weekly column to the *Miami Herald* for the Florida Keys outdoors scene. Bob's books include: *Best Restaurants of the Florida Keys, Calypso Café,* and *43 Bridges to the Florida Keys.*

MICHAEL FEDO is the author of seven published books, including *The Lynchings in Duluth, The Man From Lake Wobegon,* and the novel, *Indians in the Arborvitae.* His articles, stories, and essays have appeared in the *New York Times, Christian Science Monitor, Sports Afield, Gray's Sporting Journal, American Way, America West Airlines Magazine*, and elsewhere. He lives and fishes in Minnesota with his art teacher wife, Judy and their five grandchildren.

A graduate of Harvard Law School and former Chinese interpreter for the U.S. Department of State, **DAVID FINKELSTEIN** served for over a decade as the Ford Foundation's China specialist. Now a New York-based freelance writer, he has written for *The New Yorker, New York Times, Washington Post, L.A. Times, Field & Stream, Sports Afield, Audubon, Marlin, Atlantic Salmon Journal* and countless other national and international publications. A flamenco guitarist and avid fisherman, he also holds an 8th degree in Okinawan karate. His travel classic, *Greater Nowheres: Wanderings Across the Outback*, an account of his year in the Australian bush, was recently republished by Nick Lyons Press.

PHILLIP GENTRY is a freelance outdoor writer and photographer from Taylors, South Carolina. He has written hundreds of articles for outdoor publications throughout the Southern United States. He is also the author of the book *The Freshwater Guide to Striped Bass Fishing*, which he dedicated to his faithful dog, Jake, and is available from Knapp Press at major retail sporting goods stores.

KATHLEEN GERARD remains intrigued by the sea and all creatures therein. Her writing has appeared in various literary journals, anthologies, and has been featured on National Public Radio. Her prose has been nominated for "Best New American Voices," a national prize in literature, and awarded The Perillo Prize for Italian American Writing. She lives in northern New Jersey.

RICHARD GOODMAN is the author of *French Dirt: The Story of a Garden in the South of France* and *The Soul of Creative Writing*. He has written on a variety of subjects for many national publications, including the *New York Times, Harvard Review, Vanity Fair, Saveur, Creative Nonfiction, Louisville Review, Ascent, French Review*, and *Michigan Quarterly Review*. He teaches creative nonfiction at Spalding University's MFA writing program.

BILL HEAVEY is a bald white man who raises crabgrass in the suburbs of Arlington, Virginia. He is editor-at-large for *Field & Stream* magazine, where he writes a column, "A Sportsman's Life." He recently published a collection of his least-offensive work for *Field & Stream*, entitled *If You Didn't Bring Jerky, What Did I Just Eat?*

Veteran freelance writer **DAVE HURTEAU** has penned hundreds of articles for a variety of outdoor publications, from *Adirondack Explorer* to *Saltwater Sportsman*, where this story was first published. He has edited hundreds more during his 12-year affiliation with *Field & Stream* magazine, where as Special Projects Editor his writing recently shared in a National Magazine Award nomination. His outdoor news blog, "Field Notes," is updated daily on fieldandstream.com. Hurteau lives in upstate New York with his wife, Robin, daughter, Hannah, and son, Jackson.

The late **ROBERT H. JONES** was born in Vancouver, British Columbia in 1935. He began writing in 1975 and went full time in 1980. He contributed to over fifty different magazines, wrote three books, co-authored three more, contributed to another sixteen, edited sixteen published books, and won twenty awards for excellence in writing. He was a member of the Outdoor Writers Association of America and The Writers' Union of Canada. Jones lived in Courtenay, British Columbia.

COLIN KEARNS is the senior editor at *Field & Stream*. He graduated from Indiana University with degrees in English and journalism. A St. Louis native, Kearns has fly-fished throughout the Midwest and Montana and chased bonefish around Florida and the Bahamas. (Fortunately, none of his fishing adventures has turned into a "misadventure.") Kearns lives in New York City and has written for *Best Life* and *Salt Water Sportsman*.

MICHAEL LOVELL lives in central New Hampshire where he is a professor of Theater Arts at Colby-Sawyer College. Although he is an obsessed hunter and angler, he no longer does any fishing in the ocean out of little boats.

JOHN MEDEIROS' work has appeared in *Water-Stone Review; The Talking Stick; Gulf Coast; Willow Springs; Gents, Badboys and Barbarians: An Anthology of New Gay Male Poetry; Evergreen Chronicles; Christopher Street*; and several other journals. He has received a Minnesota State Arts Board grant; *Gulf Coast's* First Place Nonfiction Award; the AWP Intro Journals Project Award, a Jerome Foundation Grant, and several fellowships. His work has been nominated for a Puschcart Prize, and has been selected as a Notable Essay in *Best American Essays, 2006*. His website is www.jmedeiros.net.

MARY L. PEACHIN is a freelance adventure travel writer, photographer, author, and lecturer. She has published two books, *The Complete Idiot's Guide to Sharks* (Alpha/Penguin, 2003) and *Scuba Caribbean* (University Press of Florida, 2008) and is currently working on *Sport Fishing in the Caribbean* (University Press of Florida). She has also contributed to numerous publications including: *Sport Fishing Magazine, Traveling Sportsman, Destination Fish*, and *Karen Brown's Pacific Northwest*. She is the publisher of a travel adventure website: www.peachin.com.

LEN RICH is an award-winning outdoor writer living in Canada. His eighth book is due for publication in late spring 2008. He writes feature articles for numerous outdoor magazines and a popular bi-weekly newspaper column, "My Outdoors." In 1991 he received the prestigious Canada Recreational Fisheries Award. He built and operated for more than a decade a remote, fly-in trophy trout lodge in Labrador called Awesome Lake Lodge.

JOHN STRULOEFF directs the Creative Writing program at Pepperdine University in Malibu, CA. A book of his poems, *The Man I Was Supposed to Be,* is available from Loom Press. He has published in *The Atlantic Monthly, The Southern Review,* and a wide range of other magazines. A former Wallace Stegner Fellow at Stanford University, he now lives with his wife and son in the foothills of the Santa Monica Mountains.

KEITH SUTTON of Alexander, Arkansas, works full-time as a freelance writer, editor, photographer, TV personality, and lecturer. His articles and photographs appear regularly in dozens of periodicals and websites. He has written eight books, edited a dozen and co-authored more than twenty, including *Out There Fishing, Catfishing: Beyond the Basics, Hunting Arkansas, Birder's Bible,* and *Shooter's Bible.* Sutton served nineteen years as editor of the Arkansas Game & Fish Commission conservation magazine *Arkansas Wildlife.*

LOU URENECK is an outdoorsman, professor, and father. In his twenty years at Maine's *Portland Press Herald,* where he rose from reporter to editor, Lou crusaded to protect the state's environment against clear-cutting and commercial overfishing. He was an editor-in-residence at the Nieman Foundation at Harvard University and page-one editor of *The Philadelphia Inquirer.* He is now chairman of the Department of Journalism at Boston University. His work has been published in *The New York Times, The Boston Globe,* and *Field & Stream.* He lives in Brookline, Massachusetts.

MICKEY WRIGHT has lived a life full of interesting experiences. He has been a professional skier, a UPS driver, furniture salesman, teacher, health inspector, zoo keeper, prison guard (many parallels there!), wildlife control operator and park ranger. Currently, he and his wife own an environmental consulting company and a taxidermy shop. Through it all he has continued to hunt, fish, hike, boat, and camp and is passing that legacy on through his two daughters. His previous publishing experience has been writing poetry and short fiction for children. His work has appeared in publications such as *Cricket* and *Spider.* His work has also appeared recently in *Fur-Fish-Game Magazine* and *The Bird Hunting Report.*

Bibliography

Bilger, Burkhard. "Noodling for Flatheads." *Noodling for Catfish: Moonshine, Monster Catfish, and Other Southern Comforts*, Scribner, 2000.

Card, Ian (with Colin Kearns). "Out of the Blue." *Salt Water Sportsman*, November 2006. (This story has been edited and revised since its original appearance.)

Carrier, Scott. "The Greatest Fishing Story Ever Told." *Esquire*, March 2001.

DeRigne, Lauran. "Chasing Trout." *Vacations: the Good, the Bad & the Ugly, a Tall Grass Writer's Guild Anthology*, Outrider Press, 2006. (This story has been edited and revised since its original appearance.)

Epstein, Bob T. "Fit to be Tied." Originally published as "A True Account of High Jinx and Hell on the High Seas" in *Florida Keys Magazine*, 1993. (This story has been edited and revised since its original appearance.)

Fedo, Michael. "Demolition Northern Pike." Originally published as "Demolition Pike of Fish Lake," in *Lake Superior Magazine*, November/ December 1987.

Finkelstein, Dave. "Aussie Sleigh Ride." Originally published as "Meeting Jaws—Down Under" in *Sport Fishing Magazine*, February 1991. (This story has been edited and revised since its original appearance.)

Heavey, Bill. "Mongolian Prairie Dog Fishing." *Field & Stream*, December 2004.

Heavey, Bill. "Death and Fishing." *Field & Stream*, August 2006.

Heavey, Bill. "The Cuban Classic." *Field & Stream*, May 2007.

Jones, Robert H. "Appearances." *Real Outdoors*, September 1996.

Lovell, Mike (with Dave Hurteau). "Crash Course." *Saltwater Sportsman*, March 2006. (This story has been edited and revised since its original appearance.)

Peachin, Mary L. "Marlin Catches Man." Originally published as "Drowned by a Blue Marlin" in *Sport Fishing Magazine*, November 2005. (This story has been edited and revised since its original appearance.)

Struloeff, John. "The Fish Garden." *Willow Review*, Spring 2000.

Sutton, Keith. "Fishing Angola." www.espnoutdoors.com, May 2006. (This story has been edited and revised since its original appearance.)

Sutton, Keith. "Amazon Sleigh Ride." www.espnoutdoors.com, September 2001

Ureneck, Lou. "Backcast." Excerpted from *Backcast*, St. Martin's Press, 2007.

Rights

All stories are copyrighted and owned by their respective authors.